William Ames │ Technometry

The Twenty-fourth Publication in the Haney Foundation Series
University of Pennsylvania

GVLIELMI AMESII

TECHNOMETRIA,

Omnium & singularum Artium fines adæquatè circumscribens.

LONDINI,

Excudit MILO FLESHER

M DC XXXIII.

WILLIAM AMES

TECHNOMETRY

Translated
With Introduction and
Commentary by

LEE W. GIBBS

University of Pennsylvania Press
1979

Library of Congress Cataloging in Publication Data
Ames, William, 1576-1633.
    Technometry.

    (The Twenty-fourth publication in the Haney Foundation
series, University of Pennsylvania)
    Translation of Guilielmi Amesii Technometria.
    A revision of the translator's thesis, Harvard.
    Includes bibliographical references and index.
    1. Theology.   2. Philosophy.   I. Gibbs, Lee W.
II. Title.
BR118.A4513   1979   191   78-65117
ISBN 0-8122-7756-2

Frontispiece:
Original title page from William Ames, *Technometria* (London:
Milo Flescher, 1633). By permission of the British Library

Contents

Preface

This volume presents the first English translation, with an Introduction and commentary notes, of the Latin treatise on technometry written by the Puritan philosopher and theologian William Ames (1576–1633).

Scholars of seventeenth-century intellectual thought in Europe and America have rediscovered and now generally acknowledge the esteem in which Ames and his writings were held by many of his contemporaries. Those familiar with the period recognize the dominant influence exercised by Ames and his works in the history and development of Puritanism in England, the Netherlands, and especially New England. He has justifiably been called "the spiritual father of the New England churches," "the favorite theologian of early New England," and "the father of American theology."

Ames's historical importance lies in several distinct but related areas. He was one of the earliest systematizers of Calvinist theology within the philosophical framework of the French Huguenot and educational reformer Peter Ramus (Pierre de la Ramée, 1515–72). Ames was a major contributor to the development of the Covenant or Federal Theology that came to dominate Puritan thought during the latter part of the seventeenth century. He was among the first and most popular of the Puritan casuists who formulated "cases of conscience." He had a preeminent role as one of the four or five leading spokesmen and founders of independent, nonseparating Congregationalism. He was a brilliant and respected supporter of the high Calvinism of the Synod of Dort that was formulated against the Remonstrant followers of Jacob Arminius. He was a leading protagonist of Protestantism against Roman Catholicism. He stood unequaled in bequeathing to the New World his practical emphasis on living in Christian obedience to God's will.

No contribution of Ames was more important or far-reaching, however, than his formulation of an overarching, general structure of the Ramist-Puritan intellectual system. This general philosophical framework, which was really an encyclopedic outline summary of all knowledge, Ames called "technometry" (*technometria*) or "technology" (*technologia*). A systematic delineation of the nature and uses of art in general and of each of the individual liberal arts, it provided not only for the integration of theology with all of the other disciplines but also for a Ramist-Puritan critique of and substitution for traditional Aristotelian-scholastic metaphysics. Ames's technometry inspired the "technological theses" that were argued at the early Harvard and Yale commencement exercises. It provided a blueprint of knowledge for colonial New England and remained at the very center of intellectual activity in New England throughout the latter seventeenth and the early eighteenth centuries.

The appeal of technometry to the Puritan mind was grounded in its simple clarity and its all-embracing comprehensiveness. Yet the fact that this discipline grows out of the now unfamiliar Ramist teaching about the liberal arts, and the fact that most of the pertinent works are hidden away in the rare book rooms of a few privileged libraries, means that the thought form expressed in Ames's technometry remains obscure to many potentially interested readers. This present volume has been written with the intention of clarifying the strangeness and inner complexity of the thought form of technometry and of the technical terminology used to express it. Bringing to light the controlling significance of technometry in the philosophical and theological thought of Ames makes possible the correction of misinterpretations and the balancing of distortions of his thought by scholars who have been too negligent of this side of his writings. By demonstrating that technometry is the "first philosophy" from which all the rest of Ames's philosophical and theological thought flows and to which it returns, this study may serve not only as the beginning point for understanding a particular aspect of Ames's writings but also as a general introduction to his thought as a whole.

This volume on Ames's technometry also fills in one of the gaps in the dramatic development and spread of Ramist pedagogical reform during the sixteenth and seventeenth centuries. It makes available to English readers a rare and valuable treatise that played a role of great importance in a still too neglected and misunderstood chapter in the history of American thought—a chapter that remains vitally important for understanding the major motifs in contemporary American philosophy and religion. This treatise confirms Ames's place at the head of a distinctive tradition of philosophical and theological thinking that has continuously shaped the practically oriented activist spirit so characteristic of American thought from the very beginning of the English colonial period.

This volume is divided into three major parts. Part I, the Introduction, is a general essay on Ames and technometry. Section 1 of the Introduction sets forth the major events in Ames's active, tumultuous life and also gives the dates of his most important publications, thereby significantly locating his *Technometry* among the last of his published works. Section 2 surveys the principal sources of the discipline of technometry, showing that it is richly grounded in the Greek and Roman classics, in medieval pedagogy and Scholasticism, and in Renaissance humanism. Section 3 is a discussion of technometry itself: what it is, how it is structured, and how it functions throughout

Ames's thought as a whole. Section 4 delineates the short- and long-range historical influence of Ames's *Technometry* on American philosophical and religious thought by showing its impact on the technological theses debated at Harvard and Yale commencement exercises during the latter half of the seventeenth century, on the thought of Samuel Johnson of Connecticut (1696–1772), and on the thought of Jonathan Edwards (1703–58).

Parts II and III consist of a translation, with commentary notes, of *Guilielmi Amesii Technometria, Omnium et singularum Artium fines adaequate circumscribens.* The text is based upon a collation of the 1633 London edition, published by M. Flesher, and the 1651 Amsterdam edition, printed by Johannes Jansson and bound together with five other treatises that are called Ames's *Philosophemata,* or *Philosophical Treatises.* The later edition also was bound into volume 5 of Ames's *Opera, quae Latine scripsit, omnia, in quinque volumina distributa,* published by Johannes Jansson in Amsterdam in 1658. The Commentary section seeks to elucidate the meaning of the text by making cross-references to the other philosophical and theological writings of Ames; by noting parallels and differences between Ames and his classical, medieval, Renaissance, and contemporary sources; and by utilizing more recent writers insofar as they clarify the text or set forth misleading positions that need to be corrected in light of the text.

In concluding these prefatory remarks, I wish to thank those many persons to whom I have become especially indebted during my research and writing. My first debt is to my father, Norman B. Gibbs, who brought my attention to the historical importance of Ames and to the need for a study of his works. I owe much to John D. Eusden, from whom and with whom I learned much about Ames by working on the footnotes and comparing the text of his new English translation of Ames's *The Marrow of Sacred Theology* against the 1629 edition of that work. Keith L. Sprunger, who has published the definitive biography of Ames, has liberally shared both his ideas and his publications on Ames's thought and significance. Ralph Lazzaro, my esteemed former teacher of Latin and French, helped me with the translation of some of the most difficult passages of the *Technometry*. The late Douglas Horton made accessible to me parts of his fine seventeenth-century library, shared with me various aspects of his research into Ames and the unpublished translations of several of Ames's works, and carefully read and criticized my translation. I am particularly indebted to Herbert W. Richardson, who enthusiastically undertook the responsibility of thesis advisor by guiding and shaping this project on Ames in its initial stages as a doctoral dissertation at Harvard University. My work on Ames probably never would have been published had it not been discovered, befriended, and promoted by Murray G. Murphey and later by Robert Erwin, director of the University of Pennsylvania Press. The latter persuasively argued the case for my manuscript and secured the invaluable support and financial assistance of the Haney Foundation, without which publication would not have been possible. I wish to thank the staff of Houghton Library, where I spent many pleasant hours working on primary sources under one of Harvard's oldest portraits, the portrait of William Ames, and the staffs of the Andover-Harvard Library, the Folger Shakespeare Library, the Freiberger Library of Case Western Reserve University, and the Library of Cleveland State University. I am indebted to the Boston Public Library for the electroprints of the *Catalogus variorum . . . librorum . . . D. Guilielmi Amesii* (Amsterdam, 1634) and to the Yale University Library for the xeroxed copy of Ames's "Theses Physiologicae" from the student notebook of John Clark and for a microfilm copy of the same work from the student notebook of William Partridge. I am grateful to *Harvard Theological Review* (1971) and *Journal of the History of Ideas* (1972) for permission to use some of my previously published material in the Introduction. I am deeply grateful to my mother, Virginia Surber Gibbs, who shared a large part of the burden in the typing of an earlier draft of this manuscript. My wife, Joan Lawler Gibbs, has not only typed and retyped different drafts of the manuscript but has also been a faithful and loving companion in all phases of my research and writing.

L. W. G.
Cleveland, Ohio

INTRODUCTION

William Ames (1576–1633), author of *Technometry*
Dutch portrait, attributed to Willem Van der Vliet.
Courtesy of the Harvard University Portrait Collection

The Life and Works of William Ames

There are two important seventeenth-century biographies of Ames. The first, a rhetorical and laudatory account, was written in Latin by a teacher of theology at the University of Utrecht, Matthew Nethenus. Nethenus wrote a *Praefatio Introductoria* to Ames's *Opera, quae Latine scripsit, omnia, in quinque volumina distributa* (Amsterdam: Johannes Jansson, 1658). The second early life was written by John Quick in his late-seventeenth-century collection of biographies entitled "Icones Sacrae Anglicanae," which for some reason was never published and now rests in manuscript form in Dr. Williams's Library in London.[1]

There are also two more recent works on Ames with extensive biographical sections. The first is *Guilielmus Amesius, Zijn Leven en Werken* (Haarlem, 1894), written in Dutch by Hugo Visscher. The second, the only German work devoted entirely to Ames, is Karl Reuter's *Wilhelm Amesius, der führende Theologe des erwachenden reformierten Pietismus* (Buchhandlung des Erziehungsvereins Neukirchen Kreis Moers, 1940). Douglas Horton has translated the works by Nethenus, Visscher, and Reuter and gathered them into one volume entitled *William Ames, by Matthew Nethenus, Hugo Visscher, and Karl Reuter* (Cambridge, Mass.: Harvard Divinity School Library, 1965).[2] The most important and extensive recent biography of Ames, however, is Keith L. Sprunger's *The Learned Doctor Ames: Dutch Backgrounds of English and American Puritanism* (Urbana, Ill.: University of Illinois Press, 1972). Sprunger's is clearly the most authoritative life of Ames, with its fullness of detail and its portrayal of the specific cultural, ecclesiastical, political, and theological milieu in which Ames flourished and struggled. There are briefer accounts of the life of Ames in volume 2 of Benjamin Brook's *The Lives of the Puritans* (London, 1813); in volume 1 of *The Encyclopaedia Britannica,* 11th ed.; and volume 1 of *The Dictionary of National Biography,* 1921–22.

The account of Ames's life and works in this first section of the Introduction draws freely from all of these sources, following Sprunger wherever there are differences in the sources with regard to dates or specific events in Ames's life.

William Ames, better known in Europe by his Latin name, Amesius, was born in Ipswich, the chief city of Suffolk, England, in 1576, the eighteenth year of the reign of Queen Elizabeth. Ames's father, also named William, was a merchant, and his mother, Joan Snelling, was related to the families who took part in founding the colony at New Plymouth. The young Ames began his education at the local grammar school; but early in life William and his sister Elizabeth were orphaned. Ames then lived with his mother's brother, Robert Snelling of Boxford, which was only about ten miles from Ipswich. This uncle saw to Ames's further schooling until he matriculated, in 1593 or 1594, at Christ's College of Cambridge University.

Christ's College, before and after Ames was a student there, was a stronghold of nonconformity and Ramist philosophy. A number of the leaders of Elizabethan Puritanism emerged from Christ's College, including Edward Dering, Laurence Chaderton, Francis Johnson, Richard Rogers, George Johnson, Arthur Hildersham, and William Perkins. Richard Bancroft and William Covel were two graduates who were obvious exceptions to the rule. Ames received his bachelor of arts degree from Christ's College in 1598 and his master of arts degree in 1601.

Ames was immediately elected a fellow of Christ's College. Since it was required that fellows be ordained, he must have been ordained shortly before or after his election. His Puritan nonconformity led to his refusal to wear the surplice in the college chapel, and this alienated him from the master of his college, Valentine Cary. Then on Saint Thomas Day, 21 December 1609, just before the Christmas holidays, Ames preached a scathing sermon against "lusory lots" and "heathenish debauchery," condemning the card playing and dicing that were permitted during the twelve days of Christmas. Ames was summoned before the vice-chancellor and the court, and on 22 January 1610 he was suspended "from the exercise of his ecclesiastical function and from all degrees taken or to be taken." Shortly thereafter Ames "voluntarily" left his position as a fellow.

Ames accepted a call as pastor of a congregation at Colchester in Essex. Before he could be inaugurated he had to be licensed by the bishop of London, who at that time was George Abbot, soon to succeed Richard Bancroft as archbishop of Canterbury. Abbot rejected the request of Ames and the congregation at Colchester, and he further condemned Ames for preaching in his diocese without permission.

Ames despaired at the prospects for his future in England and decided to go into self-exile into the Low Countries of Holland, where many other Puritans before him had found refuge. He and Robert Parker (c. 1564–1614), who is best known for his treatise *De Politeia Ecclesiastica Christi* (1616), were sent to Holland by some wealthy English merchants for the purpose of engaging in literary controversy with the supporters of the Anglican church. Ames arrived at Rotterdam in 1610, and a few weeks later he went to Leyden, where he began to write on behalf of the Puritan cause. He soon published under his own name *Puritanismus Anglicanus* (Frankfort, 1610), a short antiprelatical and anti-Roman tract that was a Latin translation of William Bradshaw's *English Puritanisme,* published anonymously in 1605. Ames added an extensive preface in Latin to this work. Since his name alone appeared on the title page, for many years the work as a whole was often attributed to Ames.[3]

While in Leyden during 1610 and 1611, Ames was in close contact with Henry Jacob (1563–1624) and Robert Parker. These three men, along with William Bradshaw (d. 1618) and Paul Baynes (d. 1617; the successor of William Perkins as lecturer at St. Andrew's church, Cambridge, before being deprived for nonconformity), have now been identified rightly as the leading group of Puritans representing the school of *nonseparating* Independents or Congregationalists.[4] During the early seventeenth century this group of Puritans was too little known to warrant a specific name, but "contemporary writers often referred to them as 'Jacobites' or 'Amesians' because they adhered to a creed and polity which had evolved principally from the practices and teachings of Henry Jacob and Dr. William Ames."[5]

In 1610 and 1611 Ames, Henry Jacob, and Robert Parker entered into conversation with John Robinson (c. 1576–1625), pastor of the separatist congregation in Leyden, the congregation that eventually made its way to New Plymouth on the Mayflower in 1620. Ames and his associates are credited with moderating the "rigid separatism" of Robinson before he and his followers departed for the New World. There was a private exchange of letters between Ames and Robinson during 1611.[6]

At the end of 1611 Ames received and accepted a call to The Hague to become the chaplain of Sir Horace Vere, commander of English military forces and governor of Brill. While at The Hague, Ames married his first wife, the daughter of John Burgess, who had also been Vere's chaplain. When Burgess returned to England, Ames succeeded to his father-in-law's position. Ames's first wife died within a few years, leaving no children.

Around 1612 Ames became engaged in the burning theological

and political battle against Arminianism. His major opponent at this time was Nicolaus Grevinchoven (d. 1632), a pastor in Rotterdam and one of the leaders of the Remonstrants. Ames wrote his *De Arminii Sententia qua electionem omnem particularem, fidei praevisae docet inniti, Disceptatio Scholastica inter Nicolaum Grevinchovium Rotterodamamum, & Guilielmum Amesium Anglum* (Amsterdam, 1613). Grevinchoven replied with his *Dissertatio Theologica de Duabus Quaestionibus Hoc Tempore Controversis* (Rotterdam, 1615). Ames then wrote *Rescriptio Scholastica & Brevis ad Nicolai Grevinchovii Responsum illud prolixum, quod opposuit dissertationi de Redemptione Generali, & Electione ex fide praevisa* (Rotterdam, 1615). Parts of Grevinchoven's *Dissertatio* were published in Dutch translation, and Ames's *Rescriptio Scholastica* was condensed in *Guil. Amesii ad Responsum Nic. Grevenchovii Rescriptio Contracta* (Leiden, 1617).

During his employment as a chaplain at The Hague, Ames also found time to continue his dispute with John Robinson on the question of separatism. Ames wrote a *Manuduction for Mr. Robinson* (Dort, 1614), which Robinson answered in 1615 with a *Manumission to a Manuduction for Mr. Robinson.* Ames quickly responded by writing a *Second Manuduction for Mr. Robinson.* Robinson's rigidly separatist position was gradually modified, and he explicated his final position in his *Treatise of the Lawfulness of the Ministers in the Church of England,* written around 1624 but published in 1634 after both his and Ames's deaths.

Around 1618 Ames married his second wife, Joan Fletcher, who bore Ames three children, Ruth, William, and John.[7] It was about this same time that Ames was continuing his struggle against the Arminians. In 1610 a group of the disciples of Arminius had drafted a so-called Remonstrance for the States of Holland and West Friesland, directed against the high Calvinism in the Dutch Reformed church. In 1611 the States ordered the Hague Conference, which was supposed to end the controversy and prevent a schism. The famous Five Points were argued before the States: unconditional election, limited atonement, divine grace as the only cause of salvation, the irresistibility of grace, and the perseverance of the saints. No decision was reached and the controversy raged on. Ames wrote his *Coronis ad Collationem Hagiensem qua Argumenta Pastorum Hollandiae adversus Remonstrantium Quinque Articulos de Divina Praedestinatione, & capitibus ei adnexis, producta, ab horum exceptionibus vindicantur.*[8] This work came off the press and was eagerly awaited by the high Calvinists just before the convening of the Synod of Dort (November 1618–May 1619), which procured the condemnation of the Arminian "heresies."

Meanwhile, there was tremendous political and ecclesiastical pressure, instigated by James I in England and executed in Holland by the English ambassador, Sir Dudley Carleton, to remove the nonconformist Ames from his position as Vere's chaplain at The Hague. Ames was employed by the Synod of Dort to act as one of the advisors of the presiding officer of the Synod, John Bogerman of Friesland. In March 1619 Ames was finally suspended from his position as chaplain by Vere himself. Ames went to Leyden, where he hoped to be appointed to the theological faculty at the University of Leyden; positions were opening there because of the dismissal of the defeated Arminian members of the faculty. The hopes of Ames and his friends were thwarted at every move by the active resistance of the English king and his ambassador. Even when Ames tentatively agreed to fill a position teaching logic or science instead of theology, Carleton was successful in blocking his preferment "before he had given full satisfaction to his majesty."

Ames continued to live in Leyden for three years. In 1619 he was made assistant of the burse at the University of Leyden by Festus Hommius. After Hommius had been made regent of the theological college in 1619, Ames was appointed overseer of the burse. He was supported by some of the merchants in Leyden, and his duties included the superintendence over and teaching of young theological students. It was for these students that Ames began to compose his compendium of Calvinist theology, the *Medulla SS. Theologiae,* which was systematized according to the logical method of Peter Ramus. Ames dedicated this work, first published in 1623, to his merchant supporters in Leyden.

The *Medulla Theologiae* first appeared in a brief fragmentary form in 1623 as a series of disputations. The first complete edition was published in 1627. There were many subsequent editions of the *Medulla,* making it one of the most published Protestant theological treatises of the seventeenth century. The first English translations were published in 1642 and 1643 upon an order in 1641 of "a Committee appointed by the Honourable, the Commons House of Parliament for examination of Bookes, and of Licensing and Suppressing of them, &c." Ames's famous *The Marrow of Sacred Divinity* became the standard textbook for the instruction of the New England clergy throughout the seventeenth century. The favored position in which this work was held by Puritans is reflected in the words of Thomas Goodwin (1600–80), who said that "next to the Bible, he esteemed Dr. Ames his Marrow of Divinity as the best book in the world."[9] Judge Samuel Sewall of Boston tried to make the use of this work statutory and perpetual in the charter of the New Collegiate College in Connecticut.[10]

It was during the year 1621, while he was still residing in Leyden, that Ames rescued a work of Paul Baynes from oblivion, namely, *The Diocesans Tryall; Wherein all the sinnewes of Doctor Downhams Defence are brought into three heads, and orderly dissolved,* published by Dr. William Amis [Ames] (London, 1621). Baynes was a fellow at Christ's College, Cambridge, from 1600 to 1604, which means that he and Ames were colleagues there for some time.[11] After the death of William Perkins in 1602, Baynes succeeded Perkins as lecturer at St. Andrew's Church, which was just opposite Christ's College. In 1604 Baynes was suspended for his nonconformity by representatives of Archbishop Bancroft (1544–1610). Baynes's *The Diocesans Tryall* was written against the same George Downame who was a fellow of Christ's College while Ames was a student there.

Downame was numbered among the Puritans while he was at Christ's College, but later, as bishop of Derry, he became a firm Anglican. Downame is also the author of *In Petri . . . Dialecticam Commentarii,* which represents one of the important links in the Ramist tradition at Christ's College and provided one of the many sources of Ames's *Technometry.*

It was also around the year 1621 that Ames wrote his anonymous *A reply to Dr. Mortons generall defence of three nocent ceremonies; Viz. The Surplice, crosse in baptisme, and kneeling at the receiving of the sacramentall elements of bread and wine* (London, 1622). This work was written in response to the *Defense of Three Nocent Ceremonies* (1618) by Dr. Morton, bishop of Chester. John Burgess, Ames's father-in-law who was then back in England, was made responsible by Morton for the refutation of Ames's work, and Burgess eventually published *An answer Rejoyned to that much applauded Pamphlet of a nameless author* (London, 1631).

In 1622 Ames received and accepted a call to become a teacher of theology at the University of Franeker in Friesland. This appointment was opposed by Carleton, but Ames received assistance from Edward Harwood, an influential Englishman living in the Netherlands. Harwood secured Ames's appointment through intercession with Prince Maurice. On 7 May 1622 Ames gave his inaugural address, "Urim et Thummim," based on the Scriptural passage in Exodus 28:30. A few days after his inauguration Ames successfully defended before Sibrandus Lubbertus, a senior professor on the theological faculty, his "Thesibus inauguralibus Conscientia" (the initial installment of his later monumental work on conscience), and he was awarded the doctor of theology degree. On 22 August 1623 Ames delivered before the professors and students of Franeker an address entitled "Parenesis ad Studiosos." In 1626 he was appointed to the highest honorary academic office in the university, rector magnificus. He gave a rectorial address dealing with the motto of the University of Franeker, "Christo et Ecclesiae."

Ames was prolific in his writing during the years at Franeker. The books *Utriusque Epistolae divi Petri Apostoli Explicatio analytica* (Amsterdam, 1635) and *Lectiones in CL Psalmos* (1635) were remnants from his exegetical labors; they were published posthumously from manuscripts prepared for the classroom. *Christianae catecheseos sciagraphia* (Franeker, 1635) was also most probably composed during these years. In 1625 and 1626 Ames was writing the four tomes of his *Bellarminus Enervatus* against the able Jesuit apologist Robert Bellarmine. Several of Ames's shorter theological works were derived from his theological conflicts with Johannes Maccovius, his colleague in theology at the University of Franeker. These writings against Maccovius include *Disputatio Theologica de Preparatione Peccatoris ad conversionem, Assertio Theologica de Adoratione Christi,* and *Disputatio repetita, et vindicata de fidei divinae veritate.* In 1629 Ames finished his writings against the Arminians by publishing his *Anti-Synodalia Scripta, vel Animadversiones in dogmatica illa, qua Remonstrantes in Synodo Dordracena exhibuerunt & postea divulgarunt.* This work is a response to the Remonstrant version of the Synod of Dort, as described in their *Acta et Scripta Synodalia.* In 1630 he published *De conscientia et eius iure vel casibus,* which was misleadingly translated into English as *Conscience, With the Power and Cases Thereof* (London, 1641). A more accurate translation would be, "Conscience and Its Right [that is, law] or Cases."

Ames's treatise on conscience established the general formulation of Puritan morality throughout the seventeenth century. Richard Baxter, a chaplain in Oliver Cromwell's army and author of *The Holy Commonwealth* (1659), a blueprint for Puritan political theory, wrote the following in the "Advertisement" to his *Christian Directory:*

> The matter you will see in the contents: As Amesius's "Cases of Conscience" are to his "Medulla," the second and practical part of theology, so is this to be a "Methodus Theologiae" which I have not yet published. . . . And I must do myself the

right to notify the reader, that this treatise was written when I was . . . forbidden by the law to preach, and when I had been long separated far from my library and from all my books, saving an inconsiderable parcel which wandered with me, where I went. . . . For I had no one casuist but Amesius with me. . . . Long have our divines been wishing for some fuller casuistical tractate: Perkins began well; Bishop Sanderson hath done excellently *de juramento;* Amesius hath exceeded all, though briefly.[12]

In commenting on the moral philosophy component of the Harvard curriculum during the seventeenth century, S. E. Morison has made the following observation:

In addition to the study of ethics as a branch of Philosophy, the Harvard students were taught practical Ethics, or morality, in that popular manual of Protestant casuistry, William Ames *de Conscientia et eius casibus,* Englished as "Cases of Conscience." As a practical exposition of what the Word of God did and did not permit, illustrated by concrete cases, this is one of the most valuable sources of puritan morality. It was probably included with Ames's *Medulla* in the "Divinity Catecheticall" that was taught on Saturdays.[13]

Furthermore, Edwin Oviatt has pointed out that at the Collegiate School in Connecticut, Ames's *Cases of Conscience* were sometimes recited by the students in Latin on Saturdays, and that at the close of 1726 "Wollebius' 'Theology,' and Ames' 'Theses and his Medulla,' and 'the Assembly's Shorter Catechism in Latin' were recited on week days, and Dr. Ames' 'Cases of Conscience' on Sundays."[14]

Ames also supervised a series of philosophical treatises while he was at the University of Franeker. After his death six of these essays were gathered into a volume called *Philosophemata,* or *Philosophical Treatises.* These treatises were first published together in Leyden in 1643, and there were later editions published at Cambridge, England, in 1646 and at Amsterdam in 1651. The latter edition was bound into volume 5 of Ames's *Opera, quae Latine scripsit, omnia,* published at Amsterdam by Johannes Jansson in 1658.

The *Philosophemata* consists of the following treatises in the following order: (1) *Technometria, omnium et singularum artium fines adaequate circumscribens;* (2) *Alia Technometriae Delineatio, Per Quaestiones & Responsiones ad faciliorem captum instituta ac proposita;* (3) *Disputatio theologica adversus Metaphysicam;* (4) *Disputatio theologica de Perfectione SS. Scripturae, ex eius sententia ac placito;* (5) *Demonstratio Logicae Verae;* and (6) *Theses Logicae.* All of these treatises are attributed by the publishers to Ames alone on the title pages of the various editions of the *Philosophemata,* which read as follows: *GVILIELMI AMESII Magni Theologi ac Philosophi acutissimi PHILOSOPHEMATA.*

The attribution of all of these treatises to Ames's authorship has led some scholars to conclude that the two treatises on technometry and the two on Ramist logic were written by Ames, most probably when he was a student at Christ's College.[15] Yet the individual title pages show that the *Theses Logicae,* a series of 363 theses which were first published in the 1643 Leyden edition of the *Philosophemata* and compactly set forth the Ramist logic, are said to have been "once dictated to his students as matter for disputation." Furthermore, the title pages to the individual treatises reveal that at least two were written by students who were under the supervision of Ames. The *Disputatio theologica adversus Metaphysicam* was written and defended in 1629 by Peter Brest, and the *Disputatio theologica de Perfectione SS. Scripturae* is said to have been "once written and defended by William Barlae." There is even evidence that the first and longer version of *Technometria (Technometry)*[16] was written and defended during or just before 1631 by one of Ames's students named Gregory Menninger.[17] This makes it likely that the second version of *Technometria*,[18] which was first published in the 1643 Leyden edition of the *Philosophemata,* was written by Ames or one of his students shortly after 1631.

In light of the foregoing discussion, and in light of the further evidence to be presented in the next section of this Introduction, which surveys the sources of Ames's *Technometry,* it is reasonable to conclude that all of the treatises included in the *Philosophemata* did have their original inspiration and conception in the Ramism absorbed by Ames during his student days at Christ's College. Yet they were written or published toward the end of Ames's life or after his death, thereby illustrating the fact that technometry is both the beginning and the end of Ames's thought. At least three of the treatises in the *Philosophemata,* including the first version of the *Technometria,* were written in their present form by students in collaboration with and under the supervision of Ames. Nevertheless, all of these treatises, whether written by Ames himself or his students, clearly and accurately reflect and express Ames's thought as it is set forth in his other methodical and polemical treatises. Therefore, for the sake of simplicity, the lead of Ames's later publishers will be followed and all six treatises included in the *Philosophemata* will be spoken of as having been written by William Ames.

While Ames was at Franeker, Nathaniel Eaton, later to become the first president of Harvard College in the New World, wrote and defended under Ames's supervision the *Inquisitio in variantes theologorum quorundam sententias de Sabbato et die Dominico* (Franeker, 1633). It was also during those years at Franeker that Ames probably wrote or dictated his "Theses Physiologicae." The "Theses Physiologicae" were never printed, but there are at least two copies to be found in the student notebooks of two Americans. The first is found on pages 1–20 of a notebook kept by William Partridge (A.B., 1689), and the second is found on pages 37–53 of a notebook kept by John Clark (1670–1705). Both of these notebooks are now in the Yale University Library.

By 1628 Ames was under external pressure to leave Franeker. In a letter of 4 January 1629, Meinardus Scholanus, Ames's friend and colleague in theology at the university since 1626, wrote as follows:

> I perceive that a great many evils are threatening us. My fear increases because the illustrious Doctor Ames has a call. At least he has apparently resolved in his own mind, in my opinion, to go either into England or Virginia—which one I do not know. I saw a letter in which he is called to plant a church. The writer then appealed with such splendid reasoning that it would bring forth tears and be able to move a heart of iron.[19]

By December 1629 Ames was intending to set out for New England. This is known from a letter addressed to his friend John Winthrop, first governor of Massachusetts Bay Colony, to whom Ames was also related by marriage:

> HONORABLE SIRS, My dayly prayers unto God, shall bee for the good successe of the busines you have undertaken. And for my self, I long to bee with yow, though I doe not see how I should satisfie the opinion and exspectation which yow have conceyved of mee. I purpose therefor (God willing, and sending no hinderance beside what I yet know of) to come into England in sommer, and (upon the news of your safe arrivall, with good hope of prosperitie) to take the first convenient occasion of following after yow.[20]

Ames's departure was postponed, but he remained interested in the new colony and its welfare until his death. One of the reasons for this postponement was the call he received in 1632 from Hugh Peter and his church in Rotterdam. Peter had been associated with Ames at Franeker in 1628 and 1629. He later became minister of the church at Salem in New England, served as a chaplain in Cromwell's army, received custody of the library of Archbishop Laud, and was beheaded in England as a regicide in October 1660. Peter instigated Ames's call as the assistant pastor of the church and as the chief, if not the only, instructor of a new Puritan college to be established in Rotterdam. Ames did not assume his new duties in Rotterdam until the end of the school term at the University of Franeker in the summer of 1633.

Ames arrived in Rotterdam in July 1633. Here he was also associated with Thomas Hooker (c. 1586–1647). This is the Hooker who sailed in 1633 to New England, where he was first a minister of the eighth church formed in the colony of Massachusetts Bay and later of the congregation on the Connecticut River. Ames wrote his last work in collaboration with Hooker, namely, *A fresh suit against human ceremonies in Gods worship; Or a triplication unto D. Burgesse his Rejoinder for D. Morton* (Amsterdam, 1633).[21] Cotton Mather made the following notation concerning the mutual respect shared between Ames and Hooker:

> At the end of two years, he [Thomas Hooker] had a call to Rotterdam; which he the more heartily and readily accepted, because it renewed his acquaintance with his invaluable Dr. Ames, who had newly left his place in the Frisian University. With him he spent the residue of his time in Holland, and assisted him in composing some of his discourses, which are, *"His Fresh Suit against the Ceremonies"*: for such was the regard which Dr. Ames had for him, that notwithstanding his ability and experience, yet, when it came to the *marrow* of any question about the *instituted worship of God,* he would still profess himself conquered by Mr. Hooker's reason; declaring that, "though he had been acquainted with many scholars of divers notions, yet he never met with Mr. Hooker's equal, either for preaching or for disputing." And such was the regard which, on the other side, he had for Dr. Ames, that he would say, "If a scholar was but well studied in Dr. Ames his *Medulla Theologicae,* and *Casus Conscientiae,* so as to understand them thoroughly, they would make him (supposing him versed in the Scriptures) a *good divine,* though he had no more books in the world.[22]

In October 1633 the River Maas flooded a large section of Rotterdam, including Ames's house. Ames was forced to evacuate his house during the night, whereupon he contracted a cold and a high fever. In November 1633, at the age of fifty-seven, he died in the arms of his friend Hugh Peter. Peter helped see to the material and financial provision for Ames's widow and children both in Rotterdam and later in Salem, Massachusetts. So ended the life and work of "that *Phoenix* of his age, Dr. Ames,"[23] who was *intentionally* if not *eventually* a New England man:

> Know, reader, that it was by a particular *diversion* given by the hand of Heaven unto the *intentions* of that great man, Dr. William Ames, that we don't now find his name among the first in the catalogue of our New-English worthies. One of the most eminent and judicious persons that ever lived in this world, was *intentionally* a New-England man, though not *eventually*, when that *profound*, that *sublime*, that *subtil*, that *irrefragable*,—yea, that *angelical doctor*, was designing to transport himself into New England; but he was hindered by that Providence which afterwards permitted his *widow*, his *children*, and his *library*, to be translated hither.[24]

Having now established the identity and significance of the author of *Technometry*, it is in order to probe more deeply into the sources from which he drew the materials for the construction of his "first philosophy."

The Major Sources of Technometry

Anyone who approaches the writings of William Ames on technometry from the relatively recent aesthetic point of view will find it difficult, if not impossible, to understand or empathize with the theory of art and the arts that he sets forth.[25] An examination of Ames's conception of art reveals that technometry is richly grounded in Greek and Roman classics, medieval pedagogy and Scholasticism, and Renaissance humanism.

The word *technometria,* "technometry," is a transliteration into Latin from the Greek τέχνη, "art," "skill," or "craft," and μέτρον, "measure" or "survey." Technometry can thus be literally translated as "a measure or survey of art." *Technologia,* technology, which Ames uses synonymously with *technometria,* may be translated as "the theory or study of art." The Greek etymologies of these Latin transliterations show that Ames's understanding of *ars,* art, is rooted in the Greek understanding of τέχνη.

The Greeks understood τέχνη primarily in terms of a craft or a skill. One of the major sources of the Greek interpretation of art as craft or skill was Socrates. Through the mouth of Socrates, Plato lays down in his dialogues the essential framework of the classical, philosophical understanding of art.[26] This conception of art includes the following components: (a) a distinction between an end and the means to that end; (b) a distinction between a preconceived idea or thought and the activity of imposing that form or idea on some kind of matter; (c) an order where an end is conceived before the means in thought but where the means are first in execution, so that the end is attained through them; and (d) a hierarchical relation among the various arts or crafts, where one art uses what another provides so that the matter or means of one art is the finished product of another. Ames appeals to Socrates as the one through whom the liberal arts were called back from the idle speculation of the earlier "natural philosophers" to their uses in common existence, especially with respect to problems of virtue and vice, good and evil.[27]

In addition to Socrates and Plato, Ames draws upon the works of Aristotle and his interpretation of τέχνη. For Aristotle, τέχνη is artistic excellence or technical skill and also a systematic procedure for making something or a system of principles for such a procedure. He uses the verb τεχνολογέω, from which the noun τεχνολογία is derived, in the sense of "prescribe as a rule of art" or "bring under the rules of art."[28]

Ames also employs but gives his own meaning to Aristotle's five "qualities" or powers by means of which the mind (ἡ ψυχή) attains truth in affirmation or denial: scientific knowledge (ἐπιστήμη), art (τέχνη), prudence (φρόνησις), wisdom (σοφία), and intelligence or rational intuition (νοῦς).[29] These five terms in their respective Latin forms—*scientia, ars, prudentia, sapientia,* and *intellectus*—lie at the very heart of Ames's understanding of art as set forth in his theory of technometry.

Two other distinctions made by Aristotle had determinative influence on the later classical, medieval, and Renaissance (and therefore Ames's) understanding of art. The first, based on the five qualities by which the mind attains truth, is Aristotle's threefold distinction between speculative (or theoretical), practical, and poetical (or productive) sciences.[30] Art is a poetic or productive discipline, which is inferior to the speculative sciences. The second influential distinction that Aristotle made is between the liberal and the illiberal sciences and arts,[31] a distinction based on whether or not a science or art requires corporal or manual labor. There is in this classical division of the arts no separate place allotted to what are known today as the "fine arts." Sculpture and painting, for example, are classified with the servile or illiberal arts, while music is classified with such liberal arts as logic and arithmetic; the musician was thought to arrange sounds intellectually in his mind, just as the logician conceives and the mathematician numbers.

Aristotle's liberal sciences (ἐλευθερίαι ἐπιστῆμαι) formed the beginning of what the Greeks meant by "encyclopedia" (ἐγκυκλοπαιδεία or ἐκκύκλος παιδεία), that is, instruction in the whole circle or the complete system of learning and education in the liberal arts or sciences. Yet, in spite of the Greek interest in and emphasis upon encyclopedic knowledge, no ancient Greek ever composed an encyclopedia. The Romans were the first to compile the investigations of the Greeks. Important landmarks in the Roman development of the Greek understanding of encyclopedia include the *Disciplinae* of Marcus Terrentius Varro (116–27 B.C.), the *Institutia Oratoria* of Quintillian (c. 35–100 A.D.), the *Naturalis Historia* of Gaius Plinius Secundus or Pliny the Elder (c. 23–79 A.D.), the *Institutiones* of Boethius (480–524), the *Institutiones* of Cassiodorus (c. 487–583), and the *Etymologiae* or *Origenes* of Isidorus of Seville (c. 570–636). This development of "encyclopedia" out of the Greek and Roman understanding of art lies behind Ames's understanding of the encyclopedia of the liberal arts in his *Technometry*.

Ames further presupposes two significant additions by the Greek and Roman Stoics to the classical philosophical interpretation of art.[32] The Stoics made art a "system of percepts exercised together toward some end useful in life,"[33] thereby emphasizing the usefulness of art for everyday life. They also defined art as "a habit capable of making a way,"[34] thereby emphasizing not only the close synonymy between art and method (the Latin *methodus* is a transliteration of the Greek words μεθ' ὁδός) but also the fact that art is a method, a "brief way" or a shortcut to knowledge. These Stoic emphases on the utility of art for life and on art as a shortcut to comprehensive knowledge became the foundation upon which many Renaissance humanists, especially Peter Ramus, based their revolt against the pedagogical methods and understanding of the arts curriculum of the medieval scholastic tradition.

Cicero brought into the Latin tradition the Stoic interpretation of art, and the following definition is attributed to him: "Art is the bringing together of percepts exercised for leading to one end useful in life."[35] He also brought the Greek noun τεχνολογία into Latin (technologia) with the meaning of "a systematic treatment of grammar."[36] Peter Ramus later uses "technologia" in the Ciceronian sense in several of his works,[37] although he also uses the word in a broader sense, extending it to other curriculum subjects[38] and understanding it as the art of arranging the contents of the curriculum properly.

Ames's understanding of technometry is grounded, furthermore, in the arts curriculum of the medieval universities, which in turn was founded in the works of the Roman encyclopedists. The Scholasticism that developed after the rise of the medieval universities was grounded in the arts course, which from the thirteenth century on into much of the seventeenth century consisted of the so-called *trivium* (grammar, rhetoric, and logic) and *quadrivium* (arithmetic, geometry, astronomy, and music). After study in grammar and rhetoric, the study of philosophy began with logic and usually terminated with physics, although there was often some study of metaphysics and ethics or moral philosophy. A student received the master of arts degree after successfully completing his studies in grammar, rhetoric, and philosophy. After completion of the "lower" arts course, the student could, if he chose, work toward his doctorate in one of the three "higher" faculties, namely, medicine, law, or theology. The basic pedagogical methods of teaching were the lecture (that is, the reading and exposition of a written text) and the disputation. These two major forms of medieval teaching were embodied in the two major forms of writing, the commentary and questions and answers. This was the basic program of education in the universities of the later Middle Ages; in the College of Navarre in Paris, which Peter Ramus attended as a student; and in Harvard College, the first college founded by the Puritans in the New World. The Scholastics of the High Middle Ages and later composed no special treatises on the philosophy of art, but they did discuss the nature of art incidentally in connection with problems of logic, moral philosophy, and theology.[39]

All of the classical and medieval sources drawn upon by Ames converged in Renaissance humanism, which was intimately connected with a reform of pedagogical methods, arts curriculum, and literary forms of the secondary schools and universities.[40] The works on humanist pedagogy dealt both with the whole program of education in general and also with the method of presenting particular disciplines. These treatises on education formed a distinct genre of humanist prose.[41] The humanist dissatisfaction with the methods of presenting the traditional disciplines, especially the syllogistic form of argumentation and the "useless disputation" of the Schoolmen, expressed itself in the revival of Stoic doctrines. The humanists revived the Stoic definition of art as "the system of precepts [not *percepts,* as with the Stoics] exercised together toward some end useful in life." They also revived the Stoic emphasis on art as a method whereby the precepts of an art are gathered together as a shortcut to knowledge. Hence, there was a strong humanist emphasis upon "the method" of organizing or teaching an art, as well as on the speed and efficiency of mastering an art.[42]

Part of the humanist reform of the arts curriculum was the Ramist movement of the sixteenth and seventeenth centuries. The movement owes its name to Peter Ramus (1515–72), also known by his French name, Pierre de la Ramée.[43] Ramus was a Frenchman who led a stormy academic life in Paris. He was converted from Roman Catholicism to Protestantism, and he was murdered in the famous Massacre of Saint Bartholomew's Day.

Ramus inherited the passion of Renaissance humanism for method, for making the student's goal of mastering the arts easier and quicker, and for putting the arts into practical use in everyday life. He was motivated by a democratic desire to make education more easily accessible for all, and this led him into conflict with the more aristocratic tradition of medieval arts Scholasticism. Significantly, he began his reform with the *trivium* of grammar, rhetoric, and logic, the arts of communication.

Ramus first turned his attention to the reform of Aristotelian logic. He drew upon the "topical logic" of Rudolph Agricola (1444–85) and Johann Sturm, who brought the Agricolan topical logic to Paris around 1529 while Ramus was a student there. Ramus accomplished his reform of Aristotelian logic not by rejecting the whole of Aristotle's logic but by using a part of it to reinterpret the whole.[44] He added nothing new to the logic of Aristotle contained in the *Organon;*[45] he merely gave a new emphasis to part of what was already there. He made Aristotle's teaching about dialectic, set forth in *The Topics,* the key to the totality of logic. The interpreters of Aristotle's *Organon* distinguished logic from dialectic and sophistic. Logic, or apodictic, was understood to be argumentation that is syllogistic and argues necessarily from universal principles; it was based upon Aristotle's *Prior Analytics* and *Posterior Analytics.* By dialectic, based upon the *Topics,* Aristotle's interpreters meant argumentation that has at least one premise that is merely probable; dialectic can thus at best only argue persuasively. By sophistic, based upon *The Sophistical Elenchies,* Aristotle's interpreters understood an analysis of fallacious arguments.

Ramus rejected the distinction between logic and dialectic by identifying dialectic with logic, that is, by making them synonymous terms. By defining dialectic (logic) as "the art of discoursing well," Ramus modified or "reformed" Aristotelian teaching by conceiving all dialectic in terms of Aristotle's *Topics.* Ramus also refused to give the analysis of fallacious arguments (that is, sophistic based upon *The Sophistical Elenchies*) any legitimate place in the art of dialectic, for the art of dialectic is concerned only with the end and rules of true reasoning.

Ramus further reformed his logic by drawing from Ciceronian rhetoric.[46] Ciceronian rhetoric is made up of the following five parts: invention, disposition or arrangement, style or elocution, memory, and delivery. Ramus argued that the two integral parts of dialectic are invention (or the discovery of arguments) and disposition (or the arrangement of these arguments into axioms or propositions). Ramus claimed, therefore, that invention and disposition properly belong to the art of dialectic, not to the art of rhetoric. Furthermore, he argued that memory, which is intimately related to his teaching about method, properly belongs to the second part of logic, namely, disposition or arrangement. Since this left rhetoric only with style, or elocution, and delivery, Ramus and his colleague Omer Talon (c. 1510–62) wrote a new rhetoric, defined as "the art of communicating well," in the light of this new delimitation.

Ramus's final critique of Aristotle and his followers in logic was that Aristotle's logical works are not clearly methodized. Ramus regarded method as included within the second part of logic (that is, disposition or arrangement), where it was closely associated with memory. Ramus taught that method is the ordering of the universal precepts or rules of an art so that the rule that is prior and thus more general by nature always precedes that which is less known and more specific. Ramus subordinated the use of the Aristotelian syllogism to a less significant role in the second part of logic. He restricted the use of the syllogism to the function of settling a question that arises when there is obscurity with regard to the meaning of a proposition or with regard to which of two universal rules of an art is more general.

On the basis of this reform of Aristotelian logic and the correlative reform of Ciceronian rhetoric, Ramus proceeded to reform, or "methodize," the third art of the *trivium,* the art of grammar, which he defined as "the art of speaking well." He then turned his attention to reforming and modifying the arts of the *quadrivium* (arithmetic, geometry, astronomy, and music). He made arithmetic and geometry the two parts of the one art of mathematics, which he defined as "the teaching [*doctrina*] of quantifying well." Then he defined arithmetic as "the art of numbering well [discrete quantity]," and geometry as "the art of measuring well [continuous quantity or magnitude]." He relegated astronomy and music to the art of physics, which is concerned with both corporeal and incorporeal nature (that is, God, angels, and the rational soul). Ramus also ventured into the realms of "methodizing" moral philosophy in his quasi-historical-ethical treatise *Liber de Moribus veterum Gallorum* and theology in his *Commentarium de Religione Christianae*, where he begins by defining theology as "the art of living well." Hence, from his beginning with logic and rhetoric, Ramus gradually revamped the entire traditional curriculum and method of teaching. His followers soon applied his reform to the other two "higher" disciplines of medicine and law.

Ramism as a movement spread rapidly through all parts of Europe,[47] especially in Ramus's native France, the Netherlands, Germany, Scandinavia, and Switzerland. Europe was soon deluged with small, convenient school manuals in which the traditional subjects were systematically and methodically reduced to simple rules capable of being easily understood and memorized by school boys and university students. The simplicity and yet all-embracing comprehensiveness of the Ramist philosophy, along with the all-pervading emphasis on the practical utility of the arts for ends useful for everyday life, caught the imagination and mind of the rising class of practical-minded burghers and artisans. Ramus's conversion to French Calvinism and the congeniality of his method and philosophy to theology led to the adoption of his thought by many Puritans and other Calvinists who regarded Ramism as a genuinely Christian and even Calvinist philosophy.

Ramism as a movement eventually made its way to Scotland and England, where it found its most congenial acceptance at

Cambridge University, the hotbed of nonconformity and Puritanism.[48] The earliest proponent of Ramist logic at Cambridge was Laurence Chaderton (c. 1536–1604), a fellow of Christ's College from 1568 to 1577 and a close friend of the ardent Puritan Thomas Cartwright (1535–1603). Chaderton, while a reader of logic in the university's public schools, lectured on Ramus's logic. Chaderton never published anything on the subject, but he undoubtedly influenced Gabriel Harvey (c. 1550–1631), who was a student at Christ's College in 1569. In 1579, while he was praelector in rhetoric, Harvey published a series of lectures on the rhetoric of Ramus and Talon. Another writer who may well have played a decisive role in the appropriation of Ramism at Cambridge was Friedrich Beurhaus (Beurheusius). Beurhaus was a German Ramist whose textbooks on Ramus were published in London: in 1581 his *In P. Rami . . . Dialecticae Libros Duos;* in 1582 his *De P. Rami Dialecticae Praecipuis Captibus Disputationes Scholasticae;* and in 1589 his *Triumphus Logicae Ramae.*[49]

The greatest of the sixteenth-century Ramists at Cambridge was William Temple (1555–1627). Temple was a student there while Harvey was lecturing on Ramus's and Talon's rhetoric in 1575 and 1576 and while Chaderton was lecturing on Ramus's logic. He received his bachelor of arts degree from King's College in 1578, when he was elected a fellow, and his master's in 1581. He became one of the most active champions of Ramism in England by replying in 1580 to a refutation of Ramus's position by Everard Digby. Assuming the pseudonym of Francis Mildapet of Navarre, he published a tract entitled *Francisci Mildapetti Navarreni ad Everardum Digbeium Anglum admontio de unica P. Rami methodo reiectis caeteris retinenda* (London, 1580). Digby responded with another treatise, and in replying this time Temple used his own name in his *Pro Mildapetti de unica methodo defensione contra Diplodophilum* [that is, Digby], *comentatio Guilelmi Tempelii, e Regio Collegio Cantabrigiensis* (London, 1581). In 1584 Temple published at Cambridge a Latin edition of Ramus's *Dialecticae Libri Duo* together with commentary. This latter work was dedicated to Sir Philip Sidney, and Temple soon left his position at King's College to become Sidney's private secretary.

William Perkins (1558–1602) was also at least partially influenced by the Ramist movement at Cambridge. Laurence Chaderton was his tutor at Christ's College and later became a close friend. Perkins received his bachelor of arts degree from Christ's College in 1581, and his master's in 1584. He was immediately elected a fellow of his college, a position he held until 1595. This means that William Ames, who matriculated at Christ's College in 1593 or 1594, was only a student for a year or two while Perkins was a fellow. Perkins's one fully Ramistic work was written during this appointment as a fellow. He published a text entitled *Prophetica, sive de sacra et unica ratione concionandi* (Cambridge, 1592), which after his death was translated into English as *The Arte of Prophecying, or, A Treatise concerning the sacred and onely true manner and methode of Preaching*. Although Perkins does not mention Ramus as one of his authorities, the emphasis on method, the dichotomous structure of his treatise, the use of Ramus's nine artificial arguments, and the stress on axiomatical, syllogistic, or methodical disposition make it clear that Perkins is probably the first Englishman to have written on preaching within the framework of Ramist philosophy. The impact of Perkins's teaching and personal example did not cease when he left his teaching position, for he then became lecturer at St. Andrews Church, where his preaching continued to influence the students of Cambridge, especially those of Christ's College.[50] He remained at St. Andrews until his death in 1602, when he was succeeded by Paul Baynes.

Another powerful and influential Ramist who was also a fellow at Christ's College while Ames was a student there was George Downame (d. 1634). In 1616 Downame became bishop of Derry in Ireland. Just as Chaderton and Harvey probably influenced Temple and Perkins, so Temple and Perkins must have influenced Downame. Downame received his master of arts degree from Christ's College in 1581, one year after Perkins had been appointed a fellow and one year after Temple had published his text of and commentary on Ramus's *Dialecticae Libri Duo*. Downame was elected a fellow of his college and professor of logic in the university in 1585, a position he held until he was made prebendary of Chester in 1594. His teaching as professor of logic at Cambridge is reflected in the treatise he published while he was prebendary of St. Paul's Cathedral from 1598 to 1615, *Commentarii in P. Rami dialecticam, quibus ex classicis auctoribus praeceptorum Rameorum perfectio demonstratur, sensus explicatur, usus exponitur* (Frankfort, 1605).

In the midst of the thoroughly Ramist atmosphere at Cambridge while Ames was a student there, the most potent Ramist influence, at least with respect to Ames and his understanding of technometry, was Alexander Richardson.[51] Richardson, who was at Queen's College while Perkins and Downame were at Christ's, received his master of arts degree in 1587. Although he was not elected a fellow, he gave a series of lectures on various subjects. His lectures were so well received by his students and hearers that many of them wrote down his teachings and circulated them in the form of notes, which were widely read both in England and New England. The notes from his lectures on Ramist logic were printed as *The logicians School-Master; or, a comment upon Ramus Logicke* (London, 1629). Samuel Thomson, a London bookseller, published in 1657 a second edition of *The Logicians School-Master,* to which he added several sets of students' notes taken from Richardson's lectures on the rhetoric of Ramus and Talon and on physics, ethics, astronomy, and optics.[52] "The Preface or Entrance into the Book" of *The Logicians School-Master* is the closest approximation and the best guide to Ames's *Technometry* to be found in the primary literature preceding that treatise.

Finally, Ames was influenced in his understanding of art and technometry by the "systematics," those counterreformers who, although influenced by Ramus, tried to soften the implications of the Ramist reform. These men were called "systematics" because of the use of the Latin word *systema* in the titles of their works on the liberal arts. The two who are most important with respect to Ames's *Technometry* are the German scholars Bartholomew Keckermann (c. 1571–1609) of Danzig and John Henry Alsted (1588–1638) of Herborn, in Nassau. These two men remained fundamentally Aristotelian in their basic orientation. For example, they both retained the distinction between theoretical, practical, and poetical (or productive) disciplines; and they both regarded metaphysics and ethics as liberal disciplines. Therefore, Ames is in controversy with Keckermann and Alsted as much as he is indebted to them for his understanding and presentation of technometry.

Keckermann published not only "systems" of philosophy, metaphysics, physics, logic, rhetoric, and theology[53] but also what he called "precognitions" *(praecognita)* of many of these disciplines. The first volume of his collected Latin works (Geneva, 1614) begins with *Praecognitorum Philosophicorum Libri Duo,* which is followed shortly after by *Praecognitorum Logicorum Tractatus Tres,* first published at Hanau in 1604. Furthermore, in volume 2 of his collected works, Keckermann has a treatise entitled *Systematis Ethici Praecognita Generalia,* a work to which Ames refers in his *Technometry.*[54] These "precognitions" are preliminary disciplines, a propaedeutic to the study of all the arts in general and to the individual arts in particular. The treatise on philosophical precognitions sets forth Keckermann's general introduction to the study of philosophy, and the treatises on logical and ethical precognitions set forth not only the general nature of art but also the correct way to begin the study of art. Then follows the special system or method of the individual parts of art. This notion of "precognition" is crucial to Ames's *Technometry,* for he defines technometry as "the precognition of the arts."[55]

The second of the systematics, John Henry Alsted, published at Herborn in 1614 a work entitled *Logicae Systema Harmonicum,*

*in quo universus bene disserendi modus ex authoribus Perip-
ateticis juxta et Rameis traditur.* His most important work, however, was the gigantic *Encyclopaedia Septem tomis Distincta*
(Herborn, 1630). This work was published during the year, or
just before the year, that Ames's *Technometry* was composed.[56]
Alsted's *Encyclopaedia* is divided into seven volumes: (1) four
books on the precognitions of the disciplines; (2) six books on
philology; (3) ten books on theoretical philosophy; (4) four
books on practical philosophy; (5) three books on the three
higher faculties; (6) three books on the mechanical arts; and
(7) five books on the mixed disciplines. The four precognitions
of the disciplines named by Alsted in volume 1 (hexiology,
archelogy, technology, and didactic) are the four precognitions
that Ames discusses in his *Technometry*.[57]

Now that the major sources for the understanding of art pre-
supposed by Ames's theory of technometry have been brought to
light, the time has come for a more careful look at what technometry is, how it is structured, and how it functions in the
totality of Ames's thought.

The Definition, Structure, and Function of Technometry

The work of Peter Ramus was devoted primarily to the reform of the individual liberal arts. He began his reform with the medieval *trivium* of dialectic, rhetoric, and grammar, then proceeded to modify the medieval *quadrivium* of arithmetic, geometry, astronomy, and music. Ramus also gave some of his attention to ordering moral philosophy and theology methodically. But he gave very little attention to elaborating a general philosophical framework, to formulating a general philosophy of the liberal arts.[58] This task was undertaken by those who were either influenced by Ramus (especially John Henry Alsted) or by his thoroughgoing disciples (especially Alexander Richardson and William Ames). These men took Ramus's interpretation of *technologia,* the art of properly arranging the contents of the arts curriculum, and developed it further into *technometria,* an all-embracing map of human knowledge and of the intellectual roads to truth.[59]

Ames, therefore, emphatically stresses that technometry is *not* one discipline or art alongside the other liberal arts or disciplines that comprise encyclopedia.[60] Rather, he defines it as a "precognition" (*praecognitio*) of the general nature of art and of the general use of art in the activities of human life.[61] Ames's complete definition of technometry is thus as follows: *Tech-*

nometry is the precognition of the arts, which adequately cir-
cumscribes the boundaries and the ends of all the arts in general
and of all the specific, individual arts.[62] The immediate end or
goal of technometry is that of helping students to a quick and
efficient mastery of the liberal arts curriculum by preconceiving
the general nature and use of art.

The definition of technometry as "the precognition of the
arts" has nothing whatsoever to do with the later Kantian discussion about a priori prerequisites of knowledge. The preliminary
discipline of technometry is taught to students first because, in
accordance with the Ramist doctrine of method, in the order of
teaching the most general disciplines are to be taught first. But
in the order of knowing and constituting the disciplines, technometry is the last discipline to be known and constituted since
it presupposes the actual constitution and practice of all the individual liberal arts. Teachers who have mastered all of the
individual arts may then abstract the common nature or genus
of those arts (that is, the teaching about art in general) and the
universal precepts or laws that apply to art in general. Teachers
may also then try to theorize about how the individual arts are
related to each other and give a general summary of how they
are or can be used for ends useful for human life, both private
and corporate.

Ames's general definition of technometry includes and orders
or unifies all that follows in unfolding the meaning and content
of this discipline. For technometry closely follows the pattern of
the typical application of Ramist method to a discipline that is to
be taught. Ramus briefly defines method as "the disposition by
which the first known among several things is disposed in the
first place, the second in the second, the third in the third, and
so forth."[63] In short, the dictum of Ramist method is as follows:
That which is prior by nature or that which is more general
precedes. Therefore, the major parts of Ames's two treatises on
technometry explicate the general definition by further dis-

tribution, subdefinitions, and subdistributions, until the most special or specific parts of technometry have been set forth.

Ames agrees with all good Ramists in holding that the best distribution of the parts that "integrate" or make up a whole (the nature or essence of which is set forth in its definition) is a dichotomous one. His elaboration of technometry is no exception. Ames distributes technometry into the following two parts: (a) the *nature* in general of all the arts and of every individual art (theses 1–120), and (b) the *use* in general of all the arts and of every individual art (theses 121–69). This primary distribution of the integrating parts of technometry can be clearly seen in the visual chart or diagram of *Technometria,* a chart that originally appeared at the end of Ames's treatise (see Table 1). Here it is stated that "This dissertation has set forth art's nature and use." Ames then dichotomizes, or distributes further, "art's nature in general" into "art's definition" ("art is the idea of εὐπραξία, eupraxia or good action, methodically delineated by universal rules") (theses 1–87) and "art's division" (theses 88–120). It may therefore be concluded that there are three major sections or divisions of technometry. The first section deals with art's nature in general in terms of art's definition (theses 1–87); the second deals with art's nature in general in terms of its division (theses 88–120); and the third deals with art's use in general (theses 121–69).

In the section of *Technometry* dealing with the general nature of art in terms of its division, Ames concludes that there are only six arts that make up the golden chain of "encyclopedia": *logic,* the art of discoursing well; *grammar,* the art of speaking and writing well; *rhetoric,* the art of speaking and writing ornately; *mathematics,* the art of quantifying well; *physics,* the art of doing the work of nature well; and *theology,* the art (or preferably the divine doctrine or teaching) of living well.[64] Ames argues against ethics as constituting a legitimate art, for theology alone transmits the whole revealed will of God for directing human morals and

TABLE 1

DISSERTATIO ISTA
EXPOSVIT ARTIS

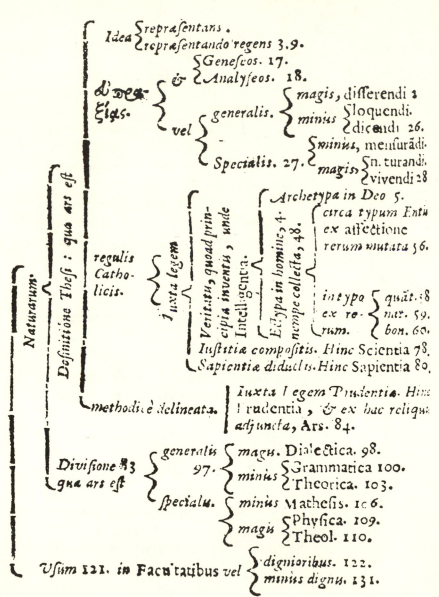

TABLE 1

This Dissertation has set forth

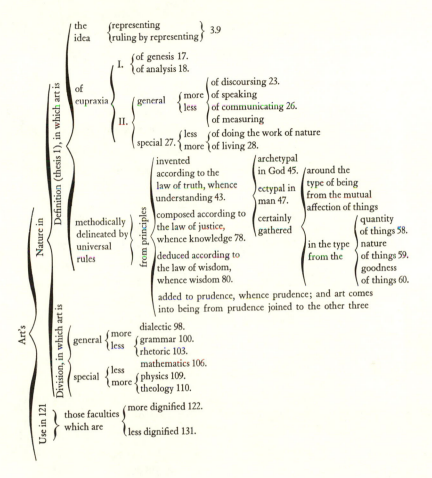

Chart of William Ames's *Technometry*

◄

Chart of Technometry from William Ames, *Technometria* (London: Milo Flescher, 1633). By permission of the British Library.

life. He also argues that household government, politics, and jurisprudence are not legitimate arts because they derive their general rules, first principles, and foundations from the art of theology.[65]

After setting forth the nature of art in terms of its definition and its division, Ames finally turns to the use in general of all the arts and of every individual art. The uses of "faculties" of the arts are dichotomized into those that are "more dignified" (the theological, jurisprudential, medical, and philosophical) and those that are "less dignified" (the so-called mechanical, manual, or illiberal arts). These less dignified faculties are all regarded as effects or uses of the arts of grammar (for example, calligraphy, typography, and brachygraphy) or of physics (for example, mining, engraving, farming, hunting, and fishing).[66]

The further development of Ramist thought into technometry or technology is the seventeenth-century equivalent of what we today would call a metadiscipline. A metadiscipline presupposes the existence of several or many individual disciplines, arts, or sciences and strives to find the common methods and criteria, or unifying principles, that govern them.[67] Technometry is the final consequence of the Ramist dictum of method, which asserts that the most general by nature should precede the more specific. It is the result of the intellectual drive to construct a general and all-inclusive philosophy of unity, a metadiscipline that systematically integrates the whole body of knowledge.

By means of the metacritical discipline of technometry, Ames attempts to overcome the sharp distinction between theoretical and practical sciences. The attack against this distinction, which Ames considered false, is implicit within the basic structuring principle of unity in his philosophy, "art." As seen above, he defines art as "the idea of *eupraxia* or good action, methodically delineated by universal rules." Although Ames is ultimately indebted to Aristotle via Ramus for this definition of art, he and other Ramists so radically modified Aristotle's teaching about the place and function of art that a new philosophical position emerged. In Aristotle and Aristotelian scholasticism, art belongs to the practical order. It is oriented toward the activity of making something and not to the pure inwardness of speculative knowledge. In art all knowledge is for the sake of guiding action rather than for its own sake. Ames modifies this Aristotelian conception of art by doing away with Aristotle's critical distinction between theoretical and practical disciplines and then by interpreting all disciplines as arts concerned with doing and making something in accordance with right rules.[68]

Ames then takes the five Aristotelian qualities or powers by means of which the mind knows and makes them various stages or levels of constituting an art or analyzing an art that has already been constituted. Understanding (*intellectus*) thus becomes the perception of the first principles or first causes of the arts; science (*scientia*) becomes the judgment of principles that have been homogeneously disposed into axioms or propositions; wisdom (*sapientia*) becomes the reciprocal distribution of axioms in appropriate levels of generality; prudence (*prudentia*) becomes the methodical ordering of the precepts or axioms of an art in a descending level of generality; and art (*ars*) is the actual execution of all the former. By utilizing this conception of art as the basic principle of his philosophy, Ames makes all human knowing practical and places all human activity under the guidance of reason.

In order to set forth the meaning and implications of this reinterpretation of art as the basic principle of unity in his philosophy, Ames presupposes and employs the model of an artificer or craftsman who makes, fashions, creates, and constructs things according to a preconceived idea and for the sake of an end. This teleological emphasis on practical ends-and-means reasoning embraces within itself the laws or precepts of "right" or "true" reason. The universal rules of art serve the function of rationally guiding the activity of the artificer by prescribing the right means and techniques for achieving his end.

Ames uses his understanding of art to explain how God creates and governs the world from rational deliberation and the exercise of free will rather than from external coercion or inherent necessity. In this Platonic perspective, God (who is also conceived of as First Being from which all other created being is derived) is primarily conceived of as the greatest Artificer.[69] God, the Master Craftsman, is thought of symbolically as first preconceiving a scope or purpose, which is primarily his glory *ad extra* among the creatures and secondarily the happiness or well-being of his creatures. Then the Divine Artisan is thought of as conceiving of the most appropriate means for achieving that end. There are many divine ideas or possibilities that God could choose. Yet some of the divine ideas or exemplars are connected and dependent on each other, thereby giving rise to a certain order. The coherent and orderly system of ideas actually chosen by God for attaining his purpose constitutes the universal principles and rules of art.

Ames proceeds to teach that art is *archetypal* in God, *entypal* in things, and *ectypal* in men.[70] Since art is one and undivided in the understanding and exercise of God, his understanding of the principles and rules of art is *archetypal*. God creates the world and then continues in his providence to govern it according to these universal rules or precepts of art. The things created by God are the image or copy of God's understanding and wisdom, thereby reflecting the cosmic order imposed upon them by God. Ames refers to these principles of art reflected in things as *entypal*. But the art that is one in the mind and exercise of God is as it were refracted in created things, so that the precepts or rules of art by means of which He creates and governs the world are perceived as manifold and various by men. The understanding of the principles of art are thus described as *ectypal* in men. Men can only perceive God's wisdom in things as manifold and by means of several arts, not by any one art. But through sense perception, observation, induction, and experience men can discover the principles and precepts of the various arts, thereby at least partially reenacting and reconstructing the coherent pattern of ideas enacted by the wisdom and good pleasure of God.

Moreover, after men have once grasped the principles and precepts of the individual arts, they may participate in their own limited way in the reality of God's artistic activity, that is, *men may imitate or make things as God the supreme Artificer makes things.* Here the teleological image of man the maker has come full circle. The idea of art originates in the specific human experience of making some artifact; then the idea is extended to the understanding of divine-natural and divine-human relations; and finally, after having been reinterpreted in terms of its cosmological setting, the image is reapplied to social life and to personal existence.

Hence, Ames's exposition of his conception of art in his treatises on technometry clearly formulates the basic principles of his ontology, epistemology, cosmology, and anthropology. Thus understood, it becomes easy to comprehend why technometry became a Puritan substitute for the traditional Aristotelian-scholastic science of metaphysics, which had been the ontological foundation of all the other arts and sciences. Metaphysics had been the "first philosophy" to consider being qua being, and it was therefore the most abstract and last science in the order of knowing and yet prior in the order of being. Ames's attack on metaphysics as a legitimate art is threefold.[71] First, metaphysics usurps the responsibility of theology in teaching about Infinite or First Being; secondly, it usurps the responsibility of logic in assigning abstract, general names or appellations to created being (that is, being derived from First Being); and thirdly, insofar as it claims to be only or purely theoretical contemplation about God, it is vain and culpable because it does not lead to practice in living well.

With this exclusion of metaphysics from the realm of the legitimate arts or sciences, the way was cleared for technometry itself to function in the place of traditional metaphysics in the philosophical system of Ames.[72] Technometry is Ames's "first philosophy," which is the most abstract and the last discipline in the order of knowing and yet prior in the order of being and teaching. It presupposes and abstracts from the individual liberal arts, and then it forms the foundation for all the other disciplines and governs them. It is the metacritical standpoint toward which all the rest of his thought tends and from which all the rest of his thought then proceeds. The result is a "Christian philosophy" that enabled many seventeenth-century Puritan intellectuals to reconcile and integrate their cosmic and rational optimism with their religious convictions relating to the sin and depravity of man and his need for supernatural grace and regeneration.[73] The impact and importance of Ames's Christian philosophy may be discerned by tracing the immediate and long-range influences of his *Technometry* in the New World.

The Influence of Technometry

Although Ames spent his life in England and Holland, his greatest impact and influence was in the New World.[74] His family emigrated to America. He was related by marriage to the first governor of Massachusetts Bay Colony, John Winthrop, with whom he was in correspondence. Some of his former students were in New England (for example, Nathaniel Eaton, the first head of Harvard College). Many of his intimate friends and great admirers were men of great importance in the New World (e.g., Hugh Peter of Salem and Thomas Hooker of Connecticut). His two sons were both attending Harvard College in 1643. At least part of his personal library became a part of the first library at Harvard,[75] and many of his own writings made up a part of Harvard's library. His works on logic, physics, and theology were used as textbooks at both Harvard and Yale.

There was another general area in which Ames, and especially his *Technometry,* had an influence that molded and unified for over a century the Puritan intellectual heritage of New England. This impact is manifested in the class of "technological theses" (*theses technologicae*). During the latter part of the seventeenth century and into the eighteenth century the technological theses made up one part of the "commencement theses" that were "posted" to be argued "against all and sundry" by graduating students of Harvard and Yale.[76] S. E. Morison has given the following general description of the "Commencement Theses and Quaestiones":

> Briefly, the theses are propositions on the seven liberal arts and other subjects studied in the undergraduate course, which any member of the graduating class, if challenged, was supposed to be able to defend, in Latin, by the recognized rules of syllogistic disputation. It was arranged beforehand, as a part of the Commencement Act, that designated students should defend certain theses, which (beginning with the sheets for 1653) are distinguished from the others by special type, or an index finger. The quaestiones were defended or opposed by candidates for the Master's degree, at Masters' Commencement on the afternoon of Commencement Day.[77]

The earliest set of specifically "technological theses" appeared on 9 August 1653 on the thesis sheet of Harvard's commencement exercises. The first technological thesis on this program reads as follows: "Art is the rule of εὐπραξία, eupraxia or good action, of being [derived] from First [Being]."[78] Technological theses appeared on the commencement program at Harvard until 1791 and at Yale until 1795. The technological theses, being most general, are always appropriately or methodically set forth before the theses dealing with the special arts.[79]

Many of the Harvard *theses technologicae* are obviously based on or drawn from the Preface to Alexander Richardson's *The Logicians School-Master* or from John Henry Alsted's *Praecognita,* which make up volume 1 of his *Encyclopaedia.* These theses differ in wording and flavor from Ames's *Technometry,* but many are taken almost verbatim from Ames. For example, the first technological thesis of 1687 is nothing other than the general definition of art with which Ames begins his *Technometry:* "Art is the idea of εὐπραξία, eupraxia or good action, methodically delineated by universal rules." Table 2 is representative of the close correspondence of many of the Harvard technological theses to theses found in Ames's *Technometry.*

TABLE 2
Comparison of Harvard Commencement Theses
and Ames's *Technometry*

Harvard Theses	*Ames's Technometry*
1678	
1. Art is the ordered gathering and combining of understanding, science, wisdom, and prudence. Cf. thesis 10 of 1691: Wisdom, prudence, science and art do not really differ.	84. This prudence, joined to understanding, science, and wisdom, renders art complete.
7. Εὐπραξία, eupraxia, is the object and end of art.	9. Art is the idea of eupraxia, having eupraxia not only as the object that the idea is concerned with representing but also as the end toward which the idea tends to direct by representing.
9. Prattomena are confused in use and separated by speculation.	36. But just as euprattomena are confused in use, so they are abstracted and separated by speculation.
10. Genesis and analysis follow each other's footsteps.	19. Each [i.e., genesis and analysis] follows the other's footsteps.
1687	
8. Practice and theory equally coincide in every art.	90. There is utterly no theoretical art, that should not have its practice. . . . Nor is there any practical art that should be learned without theory . . .

TABLE 2 (*continued*)

Harvard Theses	Ames's Technometry
1708	
6. A posterior art uses the work of a prior art.	35. A posterior art and the precept of a posterior art always use the work of a prior art. . . .

There were two specific aspects of the Harvard commencement theses upon which Ames's *Technometry*, along with his two short treatises, *Adversus Metaphysicam* and *Adversus Ethicam,* had a notable impact. First, Ames's vigorous attack against metaphysics as a discipline distinct from dialectic and theology led to the abolition of the separate classification of metaphysical theses in the Harvard commencement programs. Although metaphysics was still taught as a separate discipline at Harvard during the late seventeenth and eighteenth centuries, no separate and distinct metaphysical theses were debated after 9 August 1653—the very year in which the class of technological theses made its appearance. Theses that had before been considered as "metaphysical" from that time forth were dealt with under the headings of technology, logic, physics, and theology. Moreover, three separate technological theses from the Harvard commencement thesis sheets argue directly for Ames's position against metaphysics as a separate and distinct discipline, art, or science: "There is no metaphysics distinct from the other disciplines" (1678, thesis 15); "There is no metaphysics distinct from all the other disciplines" (1687, thesis 11); "There is no metaphysics" (1708, thesis 9). All three of these theses were especially marked for disputation as a part of the actual commencement exercises.

The second specific aspect of the Harvard commencement theses that manifests Ames's influence is the abolition of the separate classification of ethical theses. Ames's insistence that there is no legitimate, natural, moral philosophy or ethics distinct from the art of theology led to the disappearance of the previously traditional ethical theses as a part of Harvard commencement exercises.[80] The last ethical theses, at least until after 1708, appear on the thesis sheet for Harvard commencement in 1670. Here the first ethical thesis, especially marked for actual disputation, asserts that "Ethics is a species distinct from theology." Ames's position (namely, that theology alone, which draws its principles and precepts from the revealed will of God in the Holy Scriptures, teaches the principles of virtue and goodness) is the predominant view manifested in the Harvard commencement theses of the late seventeenth and the early eighteenth centuries.

The influence of Ames's thought in general and of his technometry in particular was just as powerful at Yale as it was at Harvard during this same period of time. This influence can be clearly discerned in the thought and works of Samuel Johnson of Connecticut (1696–1772). Johnson was an Anglican clergyman who was a graduate of Yale and a tutor there. He became president of King's College, later to be named Columbia University. He shared with Jonathan Edwards, one of his students at Yale, the distinction of leading the school of American idealistic philosophy.

During 1713 and 1714, while he was still a student at Yale working to fulfill the requirements for his master's degree, Johnson wrote the first version of *An Encyclopaedia of Philosophy,* which was revised and modified through several stages until it became his *Elementa Philosophica,* first printed by Benjamin Franklin in Philadelphia in 1752. Johnson gave the first version of his *Encyclopaedia* the significant title, *Technologia ceu Technometria; Ars Encyclopaedia manualis ceu philosophia.*[81] This document is the best surviving American example of a student's application of Ramist method to the whole body of human knowledge. The treatise is made up of 1,271 theses. Theses 1–63 are a rough and brief equivalent of theses 1–87 of Ames's *Technometry.* The opening theses of this section of his treatise echo Ames's work,[82] although he adds certain discussions about "First Being" and "being derived from First Being" that show his familiarity with the preface to Alexander Richardson's *The Logicians School-Master*. Johnson distinguishes between *archetypal* art, which represents and directs the divine eupraxia, and *typal* art, which is a mere shadow of the archetypal art. He further subdivides typal art into *entypal* art, which is the type of art impressed upon created things when made, and the *ectypal* art of men, the universal rules of which are gathered from created things by sense perception, observation, induction, and experience.

In dealing with the ectypal arts of men, Johnson then continues to follow Ames by dividing them into general and special rather than into theoretical and practical. But when Johnson comes to designating the general and special ectypal arts, he gives a full elaboration of each individual art, whereas Ames only briefly defines and gives the major distribution of each art in his *Technometry*. Hence, Johnson gives his own rendition and summary of Ramus's *Dialecticae Libri Duo* and Ames's *Demonstratio Logicae Verae* (theses 66–326); of Ramus's *Grammatica* (theses 414–525); of Ramist mathematics, divided into the ectypal arts of arithmetic and geometry (theses 528–776); of physics, which bears striking parallels and similarities to Ames's *Theses Physiologicae* (theses 778–999); and of theology, which is a condensed version of Ames's *Marrow of Theology* (theses 1,000–1,267).[83]

The concluding theses of Johnson's treatise reflect the discussion in theses 118 and 121–22 of Ames's *Technometry*:

> The universal comprehension of every art is rightly called discipline in a circle. Encyclopaedia is the circular comprehension of every art with respect to the subordination of ends and by means of which things emanate from and finally return to First Being. The love of encyclopaedia is philosophy. Its cognition is pansophy, because it is the cognition of all things.[84]

The last sentence of the treatise is all that Johnson wrote with regard to Ames's last section of the *Technometry* (theses 121–69) on the uses of and the faculties of using the arts: "And from these arts follow all the faculties, the higher (such as theology, jurisprudence, household economy, etc.) as well as the lower (such as all the mechanical, which are improperly called arts)."

Johnson soon rebelled against the kind of education that he had received at Yale. His changed attitude toward *Technologia ceu technometria* is revealed in two illuminating comments he inserted later in his life when he reviewed this early work. The first comment is inserted on the dedication page of the work: "N.B. When I was at College I was taught nothing but to be a conceited coxcomb like those that taught me. Indeed we had no books and our ignorance made us think almost out of our own brains."[85] The second passage is inserted at the end of the work, where Johnson had formerly written that he had finished the treatise on 11 November 1714, Thanksgiving Day's night. Johnson then added this comment: "And by next Thanksgiving, November 16, 1715, I was wholly changed to the New Learning."[86]

During the six years that he was a tutor at Yale, Johnson began to read about and was converted to the "New Learning" in science and philosophy. He read Francis Bacon (especially *The Advancement of Learning*), Robert Boyle, Isaac Newton, Descartes, and John Locke. In order to understand Newton's natural philosophy, Johnson tried to teach himself calculus and higher mathematics. He immediately introduced the "New Learning," and it is possible that it was through him that his student Jonathan Edwards came into contact with Locke.[87]

In his autobiography, written between 1768 and 1770, Johnson throws additional light upon both the educational curriculum of his college days and also upon the conservative attitude of many of his former teachers toward the "New Learning":

Mr. Fiske was a prompt man and apt to teach what he knew, but it was nothing but the scholastic cobwebs of a few little English and Dutch systems that would hardly now be taken up in the street, some of Ramus and Alsted's works was considered as the highest attainments. They heard indeed in 1714 when he [Johnson] took his bachelor's degree of a new philosophy that of late was all in vogue and of such names as *Descartes, Boyle, Locke,* and *Newton,* but they were cautioned against thinking anything of them because the new philosophy it was said would soon bring in a new divinity and corrupt the pure religion of the country, and they were not allowed to vary an ace in their thoughts from Dr. Ames's *Medulla Theologiae* and *Cases of Conscience* and Wollebius, which were the only systems of divinity that were thumbed in those days and considered with equal if not greater veneration than the Bible itself, for the contrivance of those and the like scholastical authors was to make various systems in a scientific way out of their own heads, and under each head to pick up a few texts of Scripture which seemed to sound favorably and accommodate them to their preconceived schemes.[88]

"The scholastic cobwebs of a few little English and Dutch systems," to which Johnson refers, probably include not only the work of traditional Aristotelian-scholastic logic and metaphysics but also the English and Dutch translations and versions of Ramus's logic (note that Johnson mentions Ramus by name), the work of the "systematics," such as John Henry Alsted (who is also mentioned by name), Bartholomew Keckermann, Franco Burgersdijck, and Adrian Heereboord. But the technometry or "encyclopaedia" of Alexander Richardson and of William Ames must also be included among "those English and Dutch systems," for it must be remembered that Ames was an Englishman who spent the greater part of his professional career teaching, writing, and publishing in Holland. Ames's *Marrow of Theology* and his *Conscience,* along with Wollebius's *Compendium theologiae christianae* (Basel, 1626), are cited as examples of the scholastic high Calvinism from which Johnson was defecting in the direction of the Anglicanism and Arminianism of such English divines as John Tillotson and Daniel Whitby.

Soon after his conversion to the "New Learning," Johnson encountered and became a disciple of George Berkeley (1685–1753), bishop of Cloyne in Ireland. While Berkeley lived near

Newport, Rhode Island, from January 1728 until the autumn of 1731, he and Johnson formed a close personal friendship and exchanged a series of letters discussing Berkeley's philosophical views. Johnson dedicated to Berkeley his *magnum opus,* the final edition of his *Elementa Philosophica* (Philadelphia, 1752).

One has only to look at the program and classification of the parts of learning set forth in this work to see how much Johnson had changed in his thinking from the college days when he was under the immediate influence of Ramist and Amesian works. His attention in this later work is oriented toward the introspective examination of the rise and growth of consciousness and learning. He divides encyclopedia into philology (grammar, rhetoric, oratory, history, and poetry) and philosophy. Philosophy is divided into two parts, that which deals with bodies and the natural world, that is, physics or natural philosophy, and that which deals with spirits or intelligent moral beings. The knowledge of that part of philosophy that deals with spirits or intelligent moral beings is divided into metaphysics and moral philosophy. Physics, or natural philosophy, is either general (mathematics, which includes arithmetic and geometry) or special (mechanics, geology, and astronomy). Natural history relates all the facts in nature. Metaphysics is speculative and embraces the following: logic, which includes ontology; pneumatology, which deals with men and angels; and theology, which deals with the Deity, the great Lord and Father of all. Moral philosophy (also called "natural law" or "the religion of nature") is practical and includes the following: ethics, which deals with man's conduct with respect to his attaining true happiness; household economy, which treats the prudent conduct of families; and politics, which pertains to the wise government of civil and ecclesiastical states. The facts in the moral world are related in biography and in civil and ecclesiastical history.[89]

Nevertheless, in spite of Johnson's condemnation of his earlier education at Yale, in spite of his later renunciation of Ames's rejection of the disciplines of metaphysics and ethics, and in spite of his later renunciation of Ames's rejection of the distinction between theoretical and practical disciplines, Johnson did not utterly forsake or escape the influence of his former education. Ames's synthesis of Aristotelian empiricism (whereby the principles and precepts of the arts are gathered from created things) and Neoplatonic idealism (wherein the principles and precepts of art are archetypal ideas in the mind of God) was by no means totally alien either to the empiricism and idealism of Locke and Berkeley or to the new experimental science propounded by Bacon.[90] One of the clearest examples of Johnson's fusion of his previous Ramism and Amesianism with Lockean and Berkeleyean idealism is seen in his crucial discussion of the relation of human perceptions or ideas to the archetypal ideas in the divine mind:

> The immediate Object of these our Perceptions and Actions we call *Ideas;* as this Word has been commonly defined and used by the Moderns, with whom it signifies any immediate Object of the Mind in Thinking, whether sensible or intellectual, and so is, in Effect, synonymous with the Word *Thought,* which comprehends both. —Plato, indeed, by the Word *Idea,* understood the original Exemplar of Things, whether sensible or intellectual, in the eternal Mind, conformable to which all Things exist; or the abstract Essences of Things, as being *Originals* or *Archetypes* in that infinite Intellect, of which our ideas or conceptions are a kind of Copies. . . . Not that it is to be doubted but that there are Archetypes of these sensible *Ideas* existing, external to our Minds; but then they must exist in some other Mind, and be Ideas also as well as ours; because an Idea can resemble nothing but an Idea; and an Idea ever implies in the very nature of it, Relation to a Mind perceiving it, or in which it exists. But then those Archetypes or Originals, and the Manner of their Existence in that Eternal Mind, must be entirely different from that of their existence in our Minds; as different, as the Manner of his Existence is from that of us, only by way of Sense and Imagination; and in Him as Originals; in us only as faint Copies; such as he thinks fit to communicate to us, according to such Laws and Limitations as he hath established, and such as are

sufficient to all the Purposes relating to our Well-being, in which only we are concerned. Our Ideas, therefore, can no otherwise be said to be Images or Copies of the Archetypes in the eternal Mind, than as our Souls are said to be Images of Him, or as we are said to be *made after his Image*.[91]

The same continuity of influence and yet transformation of Ramist philosophy and Puritan technometry may be argued in the case of Johnson's even more illustrious student, Jonathan Edwards (1703–58).[92] Edwards matriculated at Yale College in September 1716. He was educated in the "old" Ramist logic and philosophy before he discovered the "new" logic and philosophy of Locke.[93] The matter of Edwards's background reading and training in logical studies is intimately bound up with a comment that he made about his study of the "old logic" as opposed to "other" or "new" logic:

> One reason why, at first, before I knew other logic, I used to be mightily pleased with the study of the old logic was because it was very pleasant to see my thoughts, that before lay in my mind jumbled without any distinction, ranged into order and distributed into classes and subdivisions, so that I could tell where they all belonged and run them up to their general heads. For this logic consisted much in distributions and definitions; and their maxims have occasion to observe new and strange dependencies of ideas, and a seeming agreement of multitudes of them in the same thing, that I never observed before.[94]

Edwards was also undoubtedly familiar with, and perhaps had to memorize at least parts of, Ames's *Marrow of Theology* and his *Conscience*. And at some time before or after (most probably shortly before) reading Locke, he also was being tutored at Wethersfield in technometry or technology by Elisha Williams.

The suggestion that Edwards was familiar with and undoubtedly trained in both Ramist thought and Puritan technometry has now been well established by secondary scholarship. Yet the nature of Puritan technometry has often been misunderstood or distorted, as has the more basic nature of Ramism itself, so that Edwards scholars have not discerned clearly the importance or the continuity of the influence of either in the development of Edwards's thought. For example, Douglas J. Elwood has suggested that one likely source among others of the Christian-Neoplatonic, mystical-realist strain in Edwards's thought is Puritan technometry.[95] Elwood quotes Perry Miller as saying that Puritan technometry is "a philosophy that was nothing short of sheer Platonism." Then, drawing upon the work of Herbert W. Schneider, Elwood goes on to describe this "technologia" as "a complex theory of epistemology and metaphysics developed through the use of Peter Ramus' 'Platonic logic.' " Finally, Elwood draws upon the best known work on Ramus by Walter J. Ong to underscore the "Platonic" nature of the Ramist critique of Aristotelian logic. The first problem is that Schneider, upon whom he is dependent, has overemphasized the Platonic aspects of Ramism at the expense of the equally if not more pervasive Aristotelian aspects.[96] Secondly, Elwood's quotation of Miller with regard to the Platonic character of the theory of a preexistent platform of ideas in the mind of God omits Miller's recognition of the equally important "empirical" (and Aristotelian) emphasis upon man's coming to know those ideas through sense perception, observation, induction, and experience.[97] And thirdly, Elwood has been misled by the brilliant, exhaustive, yet flawed interpretation of Ramus by Walter J. Ong, who has also overstressed the radical dichotomy between Ramism and Aristotelian scholasticism.[98]

The important unpublished study of William S. Morris on "The Young Jonathan Edwards: A Reconstruction" is also influenced by the same flawed exaggeration of the Platonic and anti-Aristotelian character of Ramism. Furthermore, Morris refers incorrectly but repeatedly to "the anti-metaphysical logic of Peter Ramus."[99] On the one hand, Morris finds Edwards's necessary corrective of "the anti-metaphysical tendencies of Protestant Ramism" in Locke's insistence in practice, in spite of his denial in theory, of the necessary grounding of logic in metaphysics.[100] On the other hand, Morris affirms that Edwards derived his doctrine of the ontological grounding of ideas in the mind of God directly from Burgersdijck and Heereboord, who in turn had derived their ontology or metaphysics from the Spanish Jesuit, Suarez.[101] Morris then extends his interpretation of "anti-metaphysical Ramism" to Puritan technometry or technologia.[102] Finally, he misleadingly attributes this bias of Ramism and technometry to William Ames, the leading exponent of Puritan technologia.[103] The primary problem with Morris's interpretation of Ramism and Puritan technometry is that ontology or metaphysics is rejected by both only as a speculative, independent discipline; discussion of the content of traditional Aristotelian metaphysics is only to be divided up and placed within different (and for Ramism, the "proper") disciplines of logic, physics, and theology. Previous discussion has shown that Ramus, Ames, and Puritan technometry continue to speak in ontological categories, and they all ontologically ground ideas in the mind of God.

It is important to discuss briefly one other widely held interpretation of the relation between Puritan technometry and Edwards. Although Perry Miller has written one of the best and most accurate accounts of Puritan technometry in *The New England Mind: The Seventeenth Century,* he uses a series of unnecessarily biased, abusive terms to describe Edwards's estimation and rejection of technologia. Speculating that Edwards himself wrote a treatise on technologia as a requirement for his graduation in 1720, Miller concludes that "it does not survive, probably because he did not think it worth keeping."[104] Miller argues that Locke showed Edwards that "technologia was 'some of the rubbish that lies in the way of knowledge,' a 'learned but frivolous use of uncouth, affected, or unintelligible terms that had to be cleared away from the master builders.' "[105] Or again:

"The elaborate structure of technologia which was taught not as knowledge of things but of 'arguments,' collapsed in Edwards' mind like a house of cards as he learned from Locke that men can acquire the materials of reason and knowledge solely from . . . 'EXPERIENCE.' "[106] Miller also refers to "such monstrosities as technologia"[107] and to "the sterility of technologia."[108] To be sure, Edwards, like Johnson before him, reacted strongly against the then hardened and traditional Ramism and technometry. Nevertheless, in spite of Miller's disclaimer that Edwards's theology "comported with an entirely different logic, with a totally opposed metaphysic and a basically altered cosmology,"[109] much that was ancient as well as much that was modern continued to occupy the attention of Edwards. His early reading and discipline in Ramist logic and Puritan technometry continued to exert a lasting influence upon both his early and his later thought.

For example, the Puritan technometry, or technologia, in which the young Edwards was trained at Yale, was one important and abiding source of certain idealist and empiricist strains in his philosophical thought. Edwards's early essays "Of Being," "The Mind," and the so-called "Notes on Natural Science" offer the most unambiguous witness to his idealistic proclivity toward reducing all reality to states of mental consciousness.[110] The traditional dating of these early essays, especially the one entitled "The Mind," has been challenged by recent scholars, but it is generally conceded that Edwards wrote these manuscript notes mainly between 1716 and 1726, that is, during his residence at Yale.[111]

In these essays Edwards, apparently independently, reached conclusions very similar to those of Berkeley, going beyond the teachings of Locke and arguing that not only the secondary qualities of things (for example, colors, taste, smell, etc.) but also the primary qualities (for example, solidity, extension, number, figure, motion, etc.) have no existence outside of a perceiving mind:

It is now agreed upon by every knowing philosopher that colors are not really in the things—no more than pain is in the needle—but strictly nowhere else but in the mind. But yet I think that color may have an existence out of the mind with equal reason as anything in body has any existence out of the mind, beside the very substance of the body itself, which is nothing but the divine power, or rather the constant exertion of it. . . . If color exists not out of the mind, then nothing belonging to the body exists out of the mind but resistance, which is solidity; and the termination of this resistance with its relations, which is figure; and the communication of the resistance from space to space, which is motion—though the latter are nothing but modes of the former. Therefore, there is nothing else but the actual exertion of God's power, so the power can be nothing else but the constant law or method of that actual exertion. . . . The world is therefore an ideal one; and the law of creating, and succession of these ideas is constant and regular.[112]

This extension to primary qualities of the critique that Locke applied to the secondary led Edwards to the conclusion that "all existence is mental—that the existence of all exterior things is ideal";[113] that "the world, i.e., the material universe, exists nowhere but in the mind";[114] that "nothing has any existence anywhere but . . . either in created or uncreated consciousness";[115] and that the true substance of all bodies "is the infinitely exact and precise and perfectly stable idea in God's mind."[116]

The early development of Edwards's thought in this idealist direction has been and continues to be of considerable interest to scholars.[117] This development has been variously explained by the suppositions that he was acquainted with and influenced by the writings of George Berkeley; Nicolas Malebranche (1638–1715); Arthur Collier (1680–1732); the Cambridge Platonists, especially Henry More (1614–87), Ralph Cudworth (1617–88), John Norris (1657–1711), and John Smith (1616–52); and Plato (c. 428–348 B.C.). Another strain of what may be called "the older source criticism," eager to establish the claim of independence and originality, has argued that Edwards was simply a genius who, although relatively isolated in the wilderness of New England, was spontaneously led to his idealistic position simply by his own reading and reflection upon Locke's *Essay*.[118]

Without making any claims of completeness for this brief survey of older Edwards scholarship, the conclusion may safely be drawn that the enigma of the sources of Edwards's idealism has not and is not likely to be solved definitively. Most of the older suppositions have been found to be ungrounded, or at best only probable but inconclusive speculations. The growing consensus among Edwards scholars is that he was not dependent on any one author or school of thought and that the originality of his mode of argumentation and his conclusions stands out in every comparison. Nevertheless, the recognition of the continuity and yet transformation of the teachings of Puritan technometry in the thought of Edwards helps to fill in one (and *only* one) of the missing links in the development of his philosophical idealism.

The synthesis of Neoplatonic idealism and Aristotelian empiricism in Puritan technometry is also reflected in the thought of Edwards. This synthesis and the tension in his thought between a Platonic idealist metaphysics or ontology and an empiricist epistemology have long been recognized by Edwards scholars. The same early manuscript notes that are most explicit in their idealist tendencies also contain apparently countervailing emphases entailed in what has rightly been discerned as Edwards's "empiricist orientation."[119] Edwards refused to allow either his idealist metaphysics or his epistemological empiricism to degenerate into any kind of subjectivism, solipsism, or nihilism, and he did this by grounding the existence of all things in the divine consciousness or mind of God. "And indeed the secret lies here: that which truly is the substance of all bodies is the infinitely exact and precise and perfectly stable idea in God's mind."[120] Having reduced all notions of "substance" and "solidity" to the concept of "resistance," Edwards argues that there really are resistances (that is, atoms or indivisible substances) that are perceived and ordered by human perception or sensation because God has perceived them and created them in such relations. Therefore, Edwards concludes, things and their relations in the material world are what they seem to be in the representations of them derived by human sense perception.[121] An atom, or resistance, is the expression of a divine idea or reality, which in turn is "repeated" by a human idea:[122] hence, the truth of human knowledge is the agreement of the idea with existence, which in turn is the expression of the divine "idea."

Edwards's position that the natural order is real, objective, stable, and dependable in spite of (or better, precisely because of) his idealist metaphysics, along with his appeal to observation and experience, are by no means totally at odds with the Aristotelian-scholastic empiricism that is also so clearly reflected in Ames's *Technometry,* an empiricism where "there is nothing in the understanding which was not first in sense perception."

Edwards's ontological grounding of all things and of the order of the world in the divine Mind bears striking resemblance to passages from Puritan treatises on technometry. The passages in Ames's writing on the difference between God's "archetypal" understanding of the principles of art and man's "ectypal" understanding should be compared with such "idealist" passages as the following from the more mature Edwards:

> Here, by the way, we may observe the exceeding imperfection of the human understanding and one thing wherein it appears immensely below God's understanding, in that He understands Himself and all other things by the actual and immediate presence of an idea of the things understood. All his understanding is not only by actual ideas of things without ever being put to it to make use of signs instead of ideas. . . . But He has the actual ideas of things perfectly in His mind without the imperfection of that fleetingness or transitoriness that attends our ideas, and without any troublesome exertion of the mind to hold the idea there, and without the trouble we are at to have in view a number at once that we may see the relations. But He has the ideas of all things at once in His mind, and all in the highest possible perfection of clearness, and all permanently

and invariably there without any transitoriness or fading in any part.[123]

There is an even closer similarity between Edwards and Ames when the former begins to discuss God as an intelligent, designing, and voluntary agent.[124] For Edwards, God is the first (that is, efficient) and final cause of his creation. God's action in his creation and providence is teleologically directed to the attainment of a preconceived end or final cause, and his acts of creation and providence are ultimately utilitarian means of achieving that end.

Edwards's clearest expression of God as the Great Artificer or Architect who does all of his activity *ad extra* for the sake of an end is in his treatise entitled *A Dissertation concerning the End for which God created the World:*

> Indeed this affair [concerning God's ultimate end for creating the world] seems properly to be an affair of divine revelation. In order to be determined what was designed, in the creating of the astonishing fabric of the universe we behold, it becomes us to attend to, and rely on, what He has told us, who was the architect.[125]

Edwards argues in this treatise that God's ultimate end in creating the world is also the last end of all his works of providence.[126] Edwards agrees with Ames (and Calvin) in making God's chief ultimate end in creation and providence his own glory. Edwards also agrees with Ames in making God's secondary, derivative, and subordinate ultimate end the happiness of his creatures.[127] But Edwards goes far beyond Ames in defining and explicating what he understands God's glory to be, namely, that God's glory is the communication *ad extra* of the fullness of his internal glory:

> The thing signified by that name, *the glory of God,* when spoken of as the supreme and ultimate end of all God's works, is the emanation and true external expression of God's internal glory and fulness.[128]

Edwards's teleological and utilitarian ethical teaching about the nature of true virtue is concomitant with his teaching about the end for which God created the world. True virtue, which Edwards defines as "benevolence or love to being in general," is the disposition or propensity of the soul toward benevolent or loving conduct.[129]

Edwards's teaching, as set forth in the two treatises *A Dissertation concerning the End for which God created the World* and *The Nature of True Virtue,* coalesces in his *A History of the Work of Redemption,* where a basically optimistic and activistic view of nature and history is set forth. Edwards here states that the chief means chosen by God to attain the end of his glory *ad extra* is the work of redemption accomplished through the mediatorship of Jesus Christ. The work of redemption is the end of all the other creative and providential works of God. The end of the work of redemption is primarily the accomplishment of the glory of the triune God, but it is secondarily the glorification of the whole church of elect men in soul and body.[130]

Edwards believed, moreover, that there will be an era before the final judgment when the Kingdom of Christ will be established on earth. Edwards looked upon this era as a time of peace and prosperity for the Church. This vision of the Kingdom of Christ to be established on earth was not only a source of optimism with respect to the realms of nature and history but also an inspiration for men to act on behalf of the Kingdom. God's rational, moral creatures are called upon to cooperate actively with the divine activity and actually to promote the end of God's creation and providence. Hence, Edwards assured the Christian saints that God is irrevocably working out his grand design in the world and in history; at the same time, Edwards assured them of the efficacy of their own endeavors on behalf of the Kingdom. For Edwards, no less than for Ames, man can be an "imitator" of the Divine Artificer, working out his preconceived goal or great design by his works of creation, providence, and redemption.[131]

Finally, practice or exercise is just as important for Edwards as it is for Ames. Edwards asserts that the gracious, holy, spiritual affections (especially the affection of true virtue) have their exercise and fruition in Christian practice.[132] The spiritual affections arise *within* the soul through the gracious work and power of the Holy Spirit. Yet the principal *external* evidence of the possession of these spiritual affections is in the practical exercise of those holy affections. Hence, Edwards argues that Christian practice or holy living is the principal sign and evidence of the sincerity of a professing Christian to the eye of his neighbors and brethren: "By their fruits ye shall know them." He also argues that Christian practice is distinguishing and sure evidence of grace to the consciences of individuals.[133] Nevertheless, in spite of the central emphasis upon practice, Edwards—no more than Ames—does not believe in practice without understanding. Christian practice presupposes, and indeed is impossible without, an understanding profession of Christian faith:

> Though in these rules, the Christian *practice* of professors [that is, practicing Christians] be spoken of as the greatest and most distinguishing sign of their sincerity, much more evidential than their profession itself; yet a profession of Christianity is plainly presupposed. . . . That profession of these things, which is properly called a christian profession, and which must be joined with christian practice, in order to persons being entitled to the benefit of those rules, must be made . . . understandingly; that is, they must be persons that appear to have been so far instructed in the principles of religion, as to be in an ordinary capacity to *understand* the proper import of what is expressed in their profession.[134]

This brief sketch of the correlation of leading motifs in William Ames's *Technometry* in the early Yale and Harvard commencement theses and in the works of Samuel Johnson and Jonathan Edwards brings to a close the survey of the short-range historical influence upon American thought of the philosophical and theological point of view set forth in Ames's *Technometry*. In closing, a few general conclusions about the continuing long-range influence and relevance of Ames's technological point of view for contemporary American thought are in order.

Conclusion

The basically optimistic orientation of most American philosophy and theology to the rise of modern science and technology was greatly influenced by Protestantism in general and by Puritanism in particular.[135] The seventeenth-century technometry of Ames still offers more satisfactory guidelines for understanding and interpreting modern scientific technology and its cultural implications than do many modern critiques.[136] Ames's technometry, or technology (*technologia*), bridges the gap between nature and history, science and morality, theory and practice. The very essence of technology for Ames involves ends-and-means reasoning and therefore embraces goals, ideals, and purposes. Technological reason is oriented toward practical activity, and the technological act is governed by rational principles and purposes. Hence, there can be no "Big Technology" administered by morally neutral technicians.[137] For Ames, all technological activity is rational, ethical activity. Technology is oriented toward the fulfillment of goals useful to human life, and it also involves the knowledge and mastery of the procedures, skills, or techniques that serve as means to achieving those goals. Technological reason, technological activity, and technological productions are all taken up in the goal or end that is purposed. Technology is man's attempt to understand, alter, and control his natural and social environment in order to bring about certain goals.

Further, Ames has much to say about what the all-important goals or ideals that govern man's technological activity should be. The primary goal should be that of glorifying "God the Creator and Governor." God is glorified when his rational creatures study and discern his works in the natural and social realms where God himself is working to bring about his own design and purpose. God's design or goal is seen to be his own glory, which encompasses the happiness and well-being of his rational, moral creatures. Accordingly, Ames would say that by understanding what modern technology is, what it means, and how it is to be applied, man will discern God's power, wisdom, and goodness in the world and thus glorify the Creator and Governor. But the challenge of modern technology also calls man to work with God in the world to accomplish the happiness, comfort, benefit, and social welfare of all his rational creatures.

Ames tells us that man is called upon not only to become aware but also to cooperate with the design of God's creative activity. Through his own limited creativity man can participate in God's creative action. Through understanding and technology he can make the world (both natural and social) a better place. Man can strive to make his life, both individually and corporately, a work of art that will be pleasing to God, the "Great Artificer" of all things. By his technological activity man can play his small part in helping to shape and fashion a world that is ever in the process of being fashioned.

In short, Ames's *Technometry* sets forth a philosophical and theological position that provides the possibility for a basic affirmation of modern technology in all of its many facets. This treatise sets forth the possibility of an open and joyous response to the artistic, creative activity in the world of God. It sets forth the religiously-grounded moral obligation for man to know and then, in the light of that knowledge, to fashion his natural and social environment as God the Creator and Governor knows and fashions things.

Insofar as this teleological, utilitarian, or practical outlook of Ames has indeed influenced American philosophical and religious thought, and insofar as the emphasis on rational, purposeful activity teleologically oriented to some future ideal (such as the glory of God, the happiness or salvation of rational creatures, the rendering of life more reasonable, the evolution of a universal community of love, or the satisfaction of the greatest possible number of demands while destroying as few ideals as possible) remains characteristic of American philosophical and religious thought,[138] we may conclude with Matthew Nethenus, Ames's first biographer, that Ames's living influence is still with us today:

> So he being dead in the flesh yet lives. His soul lives on, now joined with the other denizens of heaven in the presence of God, whom he worshipped from his heart and in whose wars, as a good soldier of Christ, he fought with power. His body, consigned to earth, awaits the glorious and final rising of the sun of righteousness, to be raised from earth into immortal life, from contempt to eternal glory, from dreamless sleep to participation in the joys of heaven. But Ames lives even now on earth. He lives in the memory of the just men who unceasingly give thanks to God for sending so great a champion to our afflicted churches. . . . He lives and breathes in his writings through which even after his death he instructs students of orthodoxy and godliness.[139]

Notes to Introduction

1. Quick's biography of Ames has been aptly described by Keith L. Sprunger as follows: "On Dutch ecclesiastical history, Quick largely paraphrased Nethenus, but on Ames's early life in England and on his relationship to English churches in the Netherlands, Quick has important additions" (*The Learned Doctor Ames,* p. x).

2. References to these works will hereafter be made to this edition and will be cited as Nethenus, *Ames;* Visscher, *Ames;* and Reuter, *Ames.*

3. "For many years Ames was believed to be the author of the entire treatise, because his was the only name printed; the Latin version was included in Ames's *Opera* of 1658, and the English edition, although with the original short Bradshaw preface, was published in 1640 and 1641 under the name of William Ames. Finally, in 1660, the confusion was somewhat resolved by a new printing of *English Puritanisme* in Bradshaw's *Several Treatises,* this time with the preface clearly identified as the work of Ames and with the main treatise attributed to Bradshaw" (Sprunger, *The Learned Doctor Ames,* pp. 96–97).

4. "Greatest of the lot undoubtedly was Dr. William Ames (died 1633), about whom the others seem to have revolved. He was a student and friend of Baynes, was in communication with Bradshaw, and was associated with Jacob and Parker at Leyden

in 1610" (Perry Miller, *Orthodoxy in Massachusetts, 1630–1650* [Cambridge, Mass.: Harvard University Press, 1933], p. 76). For an excellent discussion of the meaning of the word "Puritanism," and for placing Ames and his colleagues within the proper context of Independent, Congregational, nonseparating Puritanism, see M. M. Knappen, *Tudor Puritanism; A Chapter in the History of Idealism* (Chicago: University of Chicago Press, 1939), pp. 2, pp. 487–93, esp. p. 493.

5. Raymond P. Stearns, *Congregationalism in the Dutch Netherlands* (Chicago: American Society of Church History, 1940), p. 3. There is another explication of Ames's contribution to Congregationalism in Sprunger's *The Learned Doctor Ames,* pp. 183–206.

6. Ames's first letter and Robinson's reply may be found in *The Works of John Robinson* (London, 1851), 3:81–89.

7. "These people went to New England with WILLIAM GOOSE, MR. of the *Mary Anne,* of Yarmouth. . . . May 11th, 1637. The examination of JOANE AMES, of Yarmouth, widow, aged 50 years, with three children, RUTH, aged 18 years, WILLIAM and JOHN, are desirous to pass for New England, and there to inhabit and remain" (John Camden Hotten, *The Original Lists of Persons of Quality . . . and Others Who Went from Great Britain To The American Plantations, 1600–1700* [New York, 1880], pp. 293–94).

8. "The *Coronis* is one of Dr. Ames's best-known works. A coronis (κορωνίς) was a stroke or a pen-flourish made by a Greek or Roman scribe at the end of a book or chapter or scene. . . . Ames's *Coronis,* published in 1618, was meant to put the 'finishing touch,' as its title indicates, to the arguments of the Calvinist representatives in the Hague Conference and thus to serve as a decisive refutation of Arminianism. It was long regarded as a well-stocked arsenal of orthodoxy" (George Lyman Kittredge, "A Note on Doctor William Ames," *Publications of the Colonial Society of Massachusetts* 13(1912):65–67).

9. Increase Mather, "To the Reader," in James Fitch, *The First Principles of the Doctrine of Christ* (Boston, 1679). In discussing the theology curriculum at Harvard in the seventeenth century, S. E. Morison states that "the favorite catechetical textbook was

William Ames's *Medulla SS. Theologiae* or Marrow of Sacred Theology, which he wrote about the year 1620 for his students at the Staaten-College in the University of Leyden" (*Harvard College in the Seventeenth Century* [Cambridge, Mass.: Harvard University Press, 1936], p. 267).

10. "A further important element in the Boston draft [of the charter] was omitted [in the draft amended by James Pierpont], wherein the Westminster Confession, as expounded in Dr. Ames' 'Medulla Theologiae' (the famous Calvinistic doctrinal book of the earlier Puritan days), was ordered 'diligently read in the Latin, and well studied by all scholars educated in the said school.' While Dr. Ames's book became one of the text-books of the Collegiate School in good season, the Pierpont founders evidently did not think it best to so order it in the charter" (Edwin Oviatt, *The Beginnings of Yale, 1701–1726* [New Haven: Yale University Press, 1916], p. 180). Nevertheless, the trustees of the college only permitted the rector to teach theology by expounding the Westminster Assembly's Latin catechism and Ames's *Theological Theses,* "and on Saturdays Dr. Ames' 'Medulla' is recited in the same tongue . . ." (ibid., pp. 199, 240).

11. Increase Mather recalls the following comment that Baynes once made with regard to Ames: "I have often thought of Mr. Paul Bayne, his farewel words to Dr. Ames, when going for Holland; Mr. Bayne, perceiving him to be a man of extraordinary parts, 'Beware (said he) of a strong head and a cold heart.' It is rare for a *Scholastical wit* to be joined with an *heart warm in religion:* but in him it was so" ("To the Reader," before *Johannes in Eremo,* in Cotton Mather, *Magnalia Christi Americana* [Hartford, 1855], 1:245).

12. *The Practical Works of Richard Baxter* (London, 1838), 1:3–4.

13. Morison, *Harvard College in the Seventeenth Century,* p. 263.

14. Oviatt, *The Beginnings of Yale,* pp. 240, 418–20.

15. For example, after mentioning the *Disputatio theologica adversus Metaphysicam* and the *Disputatio theologica de Perfectione SS. Scripturae,* Hugo Visscher says, "The other essays in the *Philosophemata,* included in his *Opera omnia,* Amst. 1658, vol.

V, were probably written in connection with his earlier education" (*Visscher,* Ames, p. 65 n. 20).

16. *Technometria, omnium et singularum artium fines adaequate circumscribens,* is the version translated and commented
upon in the present volume.

17. Robert Watt lists three independent editions of the first
version of the *Technometria* before it was bound into the 1643
Leyden edition of the *Philosophemata:* a Franeker edition in
1631, an Amsterdam edition in 1632, and a London edition
in 1633 (*Bibliotheqa Britannica* [Edinburgh, 1824], p. 26 q). In
listing the earlier editions of individual works in the *Philosophemata,* Sprunger provides the following information: " 'Technometria, omnium & singularum artium fines adaequate circumscribens,' *proponet* Gregorius Menninger, Franeker, 1631, and
under Ames's name, London, 1633; 'Adversus metaphysicam,'
subjecit Petrus Brest, Franeker, 1629, and with Ames as author
and Brest as respondent, Leiden, 1632; 'Demonstratio logicae
verae' with Ames as author, Leiden, 1632" (*The Learned Doctor
Ames,* p. 106; see also p. 80).

18. That is, *Alia Technometriae Delineatio.*

19. W. B. S. Boeles, *Frieslands Hoogeschool in het Rijks
Athenaeum te Franeker* (Leeuwarden, 1878–89), 2:119 n., translated and quoted in Sprunger, *The Learned Doctor Ames,* p. 91.

20. *Winthrop Papers* (Boston: Massachusetts Historical Society, 1931), 2:180.

21. This is the work that helped influence Richard Baxter into
his path of nonconformity; see William Orme, "The Life and
Times of Richard Baxter," in *The Practical Works of the Rev.
Richard Baxter,* 1:19–20.

22. Mather, *Magnalia,* 1:339–40.

23. Ibid., p. 310.

24. Ibid., p. 236. S. E. Morison has speculated that "there can
be little doubt that if he had lived, Ames would have been offered
the Harvard presidency" (*The Founding of Harvard College*
[Cambridge, Mass.: Harvard University Press, 1935], p. 142).

25. The relatively recent development of the "aesthetic" approach to art—an approach that emphasizes the expression of
feeling and the preeminent role of imagination—has been well

established by art historians. For example, Paul O. Kristeller has persuasively argued that "this system of the five major arts [painting, sculpture, architecture, music, and poetry], which underlies all modern aesthetics, and is so familiar to us all, is of comparatively recent origin and did not assume definite shape before the eighteenth century, although it has many ingredients which go back to classical, medieval, and Renaissance thought" (*Renaissance Thought II: Papers on Humanism and the Arts* [New York: Harper and Row, 1965], p. 165).

26. See, for example, one of the favorite dialogues of Peter Ramus and his commentators, *Phaedrus,* 271 A–C, trans. H. N. Fowler, Loeb Classical Library (Cambridge, Mass.; Harvard University Press, 1953), pp. 550–51; and *The Statesman,* 281 D–E, trans. H. N. Fowler, Loeb Classical Library (New York: G. P. Putnam's Sons, 1925), pp. 90–91.

27. Ames, *An Exhortation to the Students of Theology,* trans. Douglas Horton, 1958, no pagination. Cf. Ramus, *Scholarum Mathematicarum Liber III* (Basel, 1569), p. 77.

28. *The "Art" of Rhetoric* 1.1.9, 12, trans. J. H. Freese, Loeb Classical Library (New York: G. P. Putnam's Sons, 1912), pp. 6, 10.

29. Aristotle makes these distinctions and elaborates upon them in his *Nichomachean Ethics* 6.3–8, trans. H. Rackham, Loeb Classical Library (Cambridge, Mass.: Harvard University Press, 1945), pp. 330–73. For Ames's use and reinterpretation of these distinctions, see Prologomena to *Demonstratio Logicae Verae,* thesis 2, in *Opera, quae Latine scripsit, omnia* (Amsterdam: 1658), 5:121; also his *The Marrow of Theology,* bk. 1, chap. 7, thesis 29, trans. John D. Eusden (Boston: Pilgrim Press, 1968), pp. 96–97. All further citations of Ames's *Marrow of Theology* are to this edition.

30. *Metaphysics* 6.1, trans. Hugh Tredenick, Loeb Classical Library (New York: G. P. Putnam's Sons, 1933), pp. 292–95. Aristotle goes on to argue that physics, mathematics, and metaphysics (theology) are all speculative sciences, that metaphysics is superior to the other speculative sciences, and that the speculative sciences are superior to the nonspeculative.

31. *Politics* 8.2, trans. H. Rackham, Loeb Classical Library

(New York: G. P. Putnam's Sons, 1932), pp. 636–39. Aristotle then goes on to list the liberal arts as grammar, gymnastics, music, and (for some people) drawing.

32. These two contributions of the Stoics to the classical Greek understanding of art have been ably pointed out and discussed by Neal W. Gilbert, *Renaissance Concepts of Method* (New York: Columbia University Press, 1960), esp. pp. 11–12, 59.

33. This definition is attributed to Zeno and is found in Lucian's *Parasite,* chap. 4; see *Stoicorum Veterum Fragmenta, collagit Ioannes Ab Arnim* (Stuttgart: B. G. Teubner, 1964), 1:21.

34. This definition of art is also attributed to Zeno; see *Stoicorum Veterum Fragmenta,* 1:20.

35. "Ars est perceptionum exercitarum constructio ad unum exitum utilem vitae pertinentium" (*Stoicorum Veterum Fragmenta,* 1:21).

36. See *Letters to Atticus* 4.16, trans. E. O. Winstedt, Loeb Classical Library (New York: G. P. Putnam's Sons, 1912), 1:314.

37. Ramus, Praefatio, *De Conjugenda Eloquentia cum Philosophia,* in *Collectaneae; praefationes, epistolae, orationes* (Paris, 1577), p. 2.

38. For example, Ramus speaks of "that rhetorical technology [τεχνολογία]" in *De Sua Professione Oratio,* in *Scholae in Liberales Artes* (Basel, 1559), col. 1106.

39. Jacques Maritain has drawn together "the philosophy of art" of the Scholastics, giving special attention to Thomas Aquinas but also considering John of St. Thomas, Cajetan, and others in *Art and Scholasticism* (New York: Charles Scribner's Sons, 1942). This work shows how completely the scholastic view of art is determined by the "newly discovered" works of Aristotle; e.g., in the distinction of art as concerned with making, from science as concerned with knowing, and from practical science as concerned with doing or moral action; and in the distinction between the liberal and the illiberal (that is, manual or mechanical) arts.

40. "The term *humanista,* coined at the height of the Renaissance period, was in turn derived from an older term, that is, from the 'humanities' or *studia humanitatis.* This term was appar-

ently used in the general sense of a liberal or literary education by such ancient Roman authors as Cicero and Gellius, and this use was resumed by the Italian scholars of the late fourteenth century. By the first half of the fifteenth century, the *studia humanitatis* came to stand for a clearly defined cycle of scholarly disciplines, namely, grammar, rhetoric, history, poetry, and moral philosophy, and the study of each of these subjects was understood to include the reading and interpretation of its standard ancient writers in Latin and, to a lesser extent, in Greek" (Paul O. Kristeller, *Renaissance Thought: The Classic, Scholastic, and Humanist Strains* [New York: Harper and Row, 1961], pp. 9–10).

41. "Many of the humanists were professional tutors or school teachers, and it was through the training offered in the schools that most of the educated persons of the Renaissance period were influenced by humanist ideas, which they then carried into the larger spheres of public professional life. Hence it was natural that the humanists would be very much concerned with the tasks and problems of education. The treatises on the education of the young form a large and important genre of humanist prose, and thanks to these treatises Renaissance humanism occupies as prominent a place in the history of educational theory as in that of educational practice" (Paul O. Kristeller, "The Moral Thought of Renaissance Humanism," in *Renaissance Thought II,* p. 43).

42. "Method became the party slogan . . . for the Renaissance. An art is brought into method by being presented in short, easily memorized rules set forth in a clear manner so that the student may master the art in as short a time as possible. . . . In contrast to the rules of Terminist logic, Humanist method could be applied with profit to any of the other arts, and when so applied would speed the student on his way to mastery of the arts. . . . Thus Humanist presentations of the arts were designed to facilitate the quick and efficient learning of the subject matter" (Gilbert, *Renaissance Concepts of Method,* pp. 66, 71–72).

43. Recent interest in Ramus has been stimulated by the investigation of the scholastic and humanist background of the Puritan tradition in the United States, especially in the works of Perry

Miller and of Samuel Eliot Morison. Ramist studies have been promoted also by scholarly interest in Renaissance rhetoric, which culminated in the United States with the publication of Wilbur Samuel Howell's *Logic and Rhetoric in England, 1500–1700* (Princeton, N. J.: Princeton University Press, 1956). The most comprehensive and exhaustive study of Ramus and his thought has been carried out by Walter J. Ong in *Ramus, Method, and the Decay of Dialogue* (Cambridge, Mass.: Harvard University Press, 1958), and in his *Ramus and Talon Inventory* (Cambridge, Mass.: Harvard University Press, 1958). Father Ong has also greatly contributed to Ramist scholarship by publishing a new edition of Ramus's *Scholae in Liberales Artes* (New York: Georg Olms Verlog Hildesheim, 1970). Other approaches may be found in R. Hooykaas, *Humanisme, science et reforme: Pierre de la Ramée* (Leyden: E. J. Brill, 1958); in Christopher Hill, *Intellectual Origins of the English Revolution* (Oxford: Oxford University Press, 1965); and in Hugh Kearney, *Scholars and Gentlemen: Universities and Society in Pre-Industrial Britain, 1500–1700* (London: Faber and Faber, 1970), where Ramus and Ramism are related to the bourgeois milieu and to the rise of modern science.

44. Walter Ong has rightly noted the one-sidedness of those interpreters of Ramus who stress his anti-Aristotelianism on behalf of his Platonism, his humanism, and his interest in and reform of Ciceronian rhetoric: "Ramus' curricular reform program reveals the lines of battle drawn up between scholastic and humanist as well as the inability of either side to keep the lines completely firm. Recent close studies of Ramus have shown the tendenciousness and sheer ignorance of earlier interpretations which portrayed him as a nobly anti-Aristotelian humanist on a white charger scotching bloated scholastic dragons" (Introduction to Petrus Ramus's *Scholae in Liberales Artes*, p. vii).

45. Since the fifteenth century the following six treatises of Aristotle have been called the *Organon* of Aristotle: *The Categories* (or *The Predicaments*), *On Interpretation, The Prior Analytics* (or *Concerning Syllogism*), *The Posterior Analytics* (or *Concerning Demonstration*), *The Topics*, and *The Sophistical Elenchies*.

46. "Ciceronian rhetoric" is here taken in the broad sense set forth by W. S. Howell: "Ciceronian rhetoric exists wherever rhetoric is made to consist of all or most of the five operations anciently assigned to it by Cicero and Quintillian, these five operations being designated as invention, arrangement style, memory, and delivery" (*Logic and Rhetoric in England,* pp. 6–7).

47. The statement that Howell makes with regard to Ramism as a system of logic and rhetoric is most fitting for describing the philosophical system as a whole: "The truth is, Ramism as a system of logic and rhetoric in Latin, French, and English, is not a single unvarying doctrine but a pattern of uniformities as to general framework and a pattern of variations as to many of its details" (ibid., pp. 171–72).

48. By far the best survey of the Ramist movement is found in Howell's *Logic and Rhetoric in England,* pp. 178–246.

49. Howell points out that these three works "gave Beurhaus a larger representation in English publishing houses than any continental Ramist enjoyed during the sixteenth or seventeenth century" (ibid., p. 203). Perry Miller has rightly observed that there are many similarities and parallels between what Beurhaus was doing in his *In Paedogogiae Logicae Partem Primam Proemium* of the 1581 edition of *In Rami . . . Dialecticae Duos* and what Alexander Richardson and William Ames were doing in their writings on technometry or technology (*The New England Mind: The Seventeenth Century* [Boston: Beacon Press, 1961], pp. 158, 160).

50. Ames begins his *Conscience* with a fond reminiscence of the impact of his former teacher's preaching and example: "I gladly call to minde the time, when being yong, I heard, worthy Master PERKINS, so Preach in a great Assembly of Students, that he instructed them soundly in the Truth, stirred them up effectually to seeke after Godlinesse, made them fit for the kingdome of God; and by his owne example showed them, what things they should chiefly intend, that they might promote true Religion, in the power of it, unto Gods glory, and others salvation. And amongst other things which he Preached profitably, hee began at length to teach, How with the tongue of the Learned one might speake a word in due season to him that is

weary . . . by untying and explaining diligently, CASES OF
CONSCIENCE (as they are called). And *the Lord found him so
doing like a faithfull Servant.* Yet left he many behinde him
affected with that study; who by their godly Sermons (through
Gods assistance) made it to runne, increase, and be glorifyed
throughout *England*" ("To the Reader," in *Conscience* [London,
1641], no pagination). All further citations of Ames's *Conscience*
are to this edition.

51. Ames's immediate successors clearly regarded him as a
disciple of Richardson. For example, Cotton Mather says: "From
him [Richardson] it was that the incomparable Doctor Ames
imbibed those principles, both in *philosophy* and in *divinity,*
which afterwards not only gave clearer methods and measures
to all the liberal arts, but also fed the whole church of God with
the choicest *marrow*" (*Magnalia,* 1:336–37). Cotton Mather's
father, Increase Mather, had made a similar observation: "In
this way that great and famous Martyr of France, *Peter Ramus,*
held forth the light to others. After him succeeded the profoundly
learned and godly Alexander Richardson. . . . About the same
time the Lord raised up that great Champion, *Dr. Ames.* . . . He
in his *Medulla Theologiae* hath improved Richardsons method
and Principles to great advantage" ("To the Reader," in James
Fitch's *The first Principles of the Doctrine of Christ* [Boston,
1679]). Samuel Johnson of Connecticut draws the same line of
tradition in a manuscript synopsis of the arts that he composed
at Yale during 1713 and 1714: "The leader of the eclectic sect was
that great man, Ramus, at whose feet, as it were, there followed
Richardson and then Ames, the greatest of them, followed him
and we follow Ames" (*Technologia ceu Technometria,* in *Samuel
Johnson: His Career and Writings,* eds. Herbert and Carol
Schneider [New York: Columbia University Press, 1929],
2:60–61).

52. Thomson, in "The Book-Seller to the Reader" of this 1657
London edition of *The Logicians School-Master,* gives a glowing
account of Richardson: "The Author hereof, Mr. *Alexander
Richardson* . . . attained unto such a perfection in all Arts and
Sciences, that there is nothing almost of liberal and ingenuous
literature, which he had not in-sight into; and that such as to be

able to lay down a systeme of it in most exact and methodical Precepts . . . happy was he who could make himself Master of *Richardsons* notes. . . . But among many other Notes of his those of his Commentary on *Ramus* Logick were most generally prized and made use of by young Students . . . and indeed it was his Logick whereby, as by a Key, he opened the secrets of all other Arts and Sciences, to the admiration of all that heard him."

53. Ames possessed Keckermann's *Systema Logicum* and *Systema Theologicum* as a part of his personal library. This is known from a catalogue of his library compiled after his death, perhaps for selling the books to help ease the dire financial straits of his wife and children. See *Catalogus Variorum & insignium Librorum Clariss. & celeberrimi viri D. Guilielmi Amesii SS. Theologiae Doctoris, & Professoris olim in illust. Acad. Franekera* (Amsterdam, 1634), pp. 11, 16.

54. See *Technometry,* thesis 116, p. 114.

55. *Alia Technometriae Delineatio,* theses 1–2, in *Philosophemata* (Amsterdam, 1651), p. 45. All further page references to this treatise and the other works comprising Ames's *Philosophemata* will be to this edition.

56. There is strong internal evidence in Ames's *Technometry* to argue that he was familiar with Alsted's *Encyclopaedia*. Moreover, there is some probability that Ames knew Alsted personally. Alsted was a theologian of the Reformed church, and he was one of the German representatives at the Synod of Dort in 1618–19 while Ames was serving as advisor to the president of the synod, John Bogerman. Ames was at least familiar with some of Alsted's works, for Alsted's *Theologia Casuum* was in Ames's library (see *Catalogus, variorum . . . librorum . . . D. Guilielmi Amesii,* p. 8). Alsted was also extremely important and widely read in New England. Cotton Mather once wrote as follows: "If you would make a short Work of all the *Sciences,* and find a *North-West Passage* to them, I cannot think of any One Author, that would answer every intention so well as ALSTED. I take him, to have been as learned a Man as ever was in the World. . . ." (*Manuductio ad Ministerium, Directions For A Candidate of the Ministry* [Boston, 1726], p. 33).

57. See *Technometry,* thesis 119, pp. 115–16.

58. In his discussion of Ramist method, Alexander Richardson clearly emphasizes this neglect by Ramus of the general nature and framework of art and the arts: "This being the course of nature to proceed from the highest to the lowest, for so we must place things: the reason followeth: now indeed Ramus himself took no great pain about art in general, and therefore imagined that every definition in Art was absolutely first, but only that rule of *Encyclopaedia*" (*The Logicians School-Master*, p. 343).

59. The most important recent works that have related technometry or technology to Ames's thought include the following: Edward K. Rand, "Liberal Education in Seventeenth-Century Harvard," *New England Quarterly* 6(1933):525–51; Porter G. Perrin, "Possible Sources of *Technologia* at Early Harvard," *New England Quarterly Review* 7(1934):718–24; Samuel Eliot Morison, *Harvard College in the Seventeenth Century* (Cambridge, Mass: Harvard University Press, 1936), esp. pp. 161–64; Perry Miller, *The New England Mind: The Seventeenth Century,* esp. pp. 154–80; Herbert W. Schneider, *A History of American Philosophy* (New York: Columbia University Press, 1946), pp. 3–11; Keith L. Sprunger, "Technometria: A Prologue to Puritan Theology," *Journal of the History of Ideas* 29(1968):115–22; Keith L. Sprunger, *The Learned Doctor Ames,* pp. 105–26; Norman S. Fiering, "President Samuel Johnson and the Circle of Knowledge," *William and Mary College* 28(1971):199–236; Lee W. Gibbs, "The Puritan Natural Law Theory of William Ames," *Harvard Theological Review* 64(1971):37–57; and Lee W. Gibbs, "William Ames's Technometry," *Journal of the History of Ideas* 33(1972):617–24.

60. See *Technometry,* thesis 119, p. 115, below. In light of this exclusion of technometry from encyclopedia or the circle of liberal arts, Perry Miller is somewhat misleading when he apparently identifies the teaching of technometry or technology with the teaching of encyclopedia; see *The New England Mind: The Seventeenth Century,* p. 121.

61. "By what preparation must you be instructed so that you may become skillful in the arts? By a threefold preparation, namely, by the precognition [*praecognitione*], cognition [*cognitione*], and recognition [*recognitione*] of the arts." "What is

to be generally preconceived [*praecognoscendum est*] by you so that you may easily learn and attain the arts? It is necessary to foreknow [*praenosse*] technometry" (*Alia Technometriae Delineatio,* theses 1–2, p. 45). Ames's definition of technometry or technology as a precognition of the arts should be compared with the notion of *praecognita* in John Henry Alsted, *Encyclopaedia Septem tomis distincta,* Vol. 1, bk. 1, pt. 1 (Herborn, 1630), p. 50; and Bartholomew Keckermann, *Praecognitorum Philosophicorum Libri Duo,* in *Opera Omnia* (Geneva, 1614), vol. 1, col. 5. Ames differed from Alsted and Keckermann only in holding that there is one precognition of the arts (namely, technometry) and not several as these men believed; see *Technometry,* thesis 119, p. 115.

62. The complete definition of what Ames means by technometry must be derived by putting together his preliminary definition of technometry in *Alia Technometriae Delineatio,* namely, "technometry is the precognition of the arts," with the title of the first version of *Technometria,* namely, "Technometry, which adequately circumscribes the Boundaries and the Ends of all the Arts and of every individual Art." What Alexander Richardson says about Ramus's definition of the art of dialectic is true of Ramist definitions of the arts in general—they are defined in terms of their ends: "So here our Author desireth to give us the form of reason, which because he cannot do, therefore he delivers by the final cause, the next act to the form; so that when he saith *dialectica est ars bene disserendi,* he means it is such an art that hath such a form that doth *bene disserere* . . ." (*The Logicians School-Master,* p. 39).

63. Ramus, *Dialectique* (1555), notes et commentaire de Michel Dassonville (Geneva, 1964), p. 144.

64. "These six arts perfect the whole man: logic directing his intellect; theology his will; and the remaining arts (grammar, rhetoric, mathematics, and physics) his locomotion according to rule in their eupraxiae. With these six arts, the circle or encyclopedia of education and the arts is most perfectly completed and finished, receiving neither more nor less arts" (*Technometry,* theses 117–18, p. 115 below).

65. Ibid., theses 113–16, pp. 113–15.

66. Ibid., theses 131–66, pp. 118–25.

67. Herbert W. Richardson has given the following suggestive description of the emergence and characteristics of the contemporary metadisciplines: "The distinguishing trait of twentieth-century intellectual life is the emergence and proliferation of the 'meta-disciplines' (or 'meta-sciences'): e.g., meta-mathematics, meta-logic, meta-ethics, meta-jurisprudence, meta-politics, meta-theater, meta-language (hermeneutics and linguistic analysis), meta-sociology (sociology of knowledge), and so on. The emergence of these meta-disciplines signifies a fundamental change in human orientation. We may compare this contemporary movement with the development in the eighteenth and nineteenth centuries of the special sciences as self-contained disciplines: chemistry, biology, botany, geology, history, psychology, and so forth. Whereas this earlier period proliferated special sciences through the application of rigorous techniques which critically reduced (and therefore multiplied) the objects of science *per se,* the characteristic of contemporary intellectual life is the proliferation of meta-disciplines through the critical analysis of the methods and presuppositions of the special sciences themselves" (*Toward an American Theology* [New York: Harper and Row, 1967], pp. 71–72).

68. *Technometry,* theses 88–95, pp. 108–10.

69. See Ames, *The Substance of Christian Religion* (London, 1659), pp. 65–67; also *The Marrow of Theology,* bk. I, chap. 7, theses 11–23, pp. 95–96.

70. *Technometry,* theses 45–48, pp. 100–101; *Alia Technometriae Delineatio,* theses 51–53, pp. 57–58.

71. *Technometry,* theses 51–53, 91, pp. 101–2, 109; also Ames's treatise in *Philosophemata* entitled *Disputatio theologica adversus metaphysicam,* in *Opera . . . omnia,* 5:85–97. For an account of the furor raised between Ramists and Aristotelians at the University of Franeker because of the debate instigated by the content of this treatise against metaphysics, see Sprunger, *The Learned Doctor Ames,* p. 82.

72. The typographer's preface to Ames's *Philosophemata* makes this point with respect to the two treatises *Adversus Metaphysicam* and *Adversus Ethicam.* The typographer's observation may

be extended to all of Ames's other writings and to his thought as a whole: "We present to you, benevolent reader, the philosophical treatises of that most celebrated man, Dr. William Ames, who was of disciplined and solid judgment not only in those theological and logical writings which are still in existence, but also in philosophical writings, as these treatises which we now give to you will abundantly demonstrate. We put *Technometry* first for you, which is simple in argument and two-fold in form. Either of these forms of *Technometry* will accurately prescribe the limits and the ends of the disciplines and faculties. In the first form, all things are said more concisely and the light there is more contracted, for in the second form *Technometry* is explained more diffusely and more broadly through questions. The disputations *Against Metaphysics* and *Against Ethics* are subjected to the two-fold *Technometry*. For the author proscribes both metaphysics and ethics from the realm and fruits of philosophy by reasons of no small weight, and in *Technology* he banishes them to their place in other disciplines." Typographus Lectori, in *Guilielmi Amesii . . . Philosophemata* (Amsterdam, 1651).

73. Perry Miller has made the following excellent summary of many of the basic achievements of Puritan technometry or technology: "The most important point, speaking historically, is that through it [*technologia*] Puritans secured everything their hearts desired in the realm of philosophy. . . . It accounted for an intelligible universe without infringing the sovereignty of God; it showed how men could apprehend the intelligibles, even in a state of sin, by an immediate and instantaneous recognition. It proved that intelligibles exist objectively, not in man's head but in the thing. It allowed men to glory in the possession of innate powers without giving them cause to conclude that grace was superfluous. It provided a philosophical account of the visible universe, of its nature and its origin, that was thoroughly compatible with the theology, which it supplemented and supported. It demonstrated that by an innate power or an inherent habit of methodical apprehension men could perceive the eternal and divine rules upon which the natural world is constructed, and that the sum total of this knowledge was a unified and coherent organon. It provided a framework in which the Puritan, while

remaining a man of piety and a believer in original sin and irresistible grace, could stabilize his intellectual heritage" (*The New England Mind: The Seventeenth Century,* pp. 175–76).

74. John D. Eusden has noted that Ames's "influence was far greater in Holland and in the New World than in his native England . . ." (*Puritans, Lawyers, and Politics* [New Haven: Yale University Press, 1958], p. 14 n. 6). Hugo Visscher has explained Ames's later obscurity in the Netherlands: "The question arises: how it is possible that Ames, notwithstanding his great significance, is only rarely mentioned in the history of our church? Indeed, his name is not generally known. . . . This can be explained by the fact that he was an alien and so does not come to the foreground in Dutch history. . . . He did not know enough Dutch to write in it and his works in Latin for the most part defied translation. An attempt was once made to translate the *Medulla* and the *Casus Conscientiae* into Dutch. . . . Even in translation the text appears not to have been translated. . . . Ames's *Medulla* was too compact, too academic for the general public. He demanded much of his readers. For this reason, although it did not get lost completely, it remained in the background. It was pushed aside by what others wrote. This applies to the *Medulla* and in greater or less degree is also applicable to his other works" (Visscher, *Ames,* pp. 146–47).

75. Cotton Mather's claim that Ames's library found its way to the New World has been challenged by recent scholars; see Samuel Eliot Morison, *The Founding of Harvard College* (Cambridge, Mass.: Harvard University Press, 1935), p. 267, and Sprunger, *The Learned Doctor Ames,* pp. 255–56. For an older but different argument that at least partially defends Mather's position, see Julius H. Tuttle, "Library of Dr. William Ames," *Publications of the Colonial Society of Massachusetts* 14(1911):63–66.

76. S. E. Morison has conveniently gathered the full text of all Harvard "Commencement Theses and Quaestiones," of which copies have survived from 1643–1708; see *Harvard College in the Seventeenth Century,* 2:583–638. All further citations from the Harvard technological theses are to this source.

77. Ibid., p. 580.

78. Ibid., p. 589.

79. E. K. Rand was the first to notice and raise questions about the nature and source of the technological theses as a part of the curriculum of early Harvard. He closed his article with the following questions: "From what source did President Dunster take the term technology in the sense that these ancient programs reveal? Or did he himself invent it? What modern dictionary has taken account of that meaning? How long did it last? If anybody is interested in a really startling reform, let me suggest, in closing, that he might found a new Massachusetts Institute of Technology—in the ancient sense of that term" ("Liberal Education in Seventeenth-Century Harvard," *The New England Quarterly* 6[1933]:550–51; see also the section on "Theses Technologicae" in Morison, *Harvard College in the Seventeenth Century,* 2:534–41). Porter G. Perrin made an initial attempt to answer Rand's questions by pointing to Ames's *Technometry* and the *Praecognita* of Alsted's *Encyclopaedia* as likely sources of the technological theses ("Possible Sources of *Technologia* at Early Harvard," *The New England Quarterly* 7[1934]:718–24). In 1936 S. E. Morison confirmed Ames and Alsted as two of the authors who were sources of Harvard technological theses, and he added Alexander Richardson's *The Logicians School-Master* as a third source (*Harvard College in the Seventeenth Century,* 2:161–64). In 1939 Perry Miller utilized the works of these men and added the insights of his own research to trace lines of influence from the works of Peter Ramus to Richardson, Ames, and Alsted (*The New England Mind: The Seventeenth Century,* pp. 154–80). More recent works dealing with the subject of technometry or technology have added relatively little to the findings of these scholars.

80. This position is taken against that of S. E. Morison and Perry Miller. Morison and Miller argue that Harvard rejected Ames on this point and followed Bartholomew Keckermann, who argued that ethics, or moral philosophy, and theology are distinct disciplines since their ends are different; that is, ethics is concerned with the exterior civil and social values dealing with this life, while theology is concerned with interior religious virtues leading to eternal happiness (Morison, *Harvard College in the Seventeenth Century,* 1:260; Miller, *The New England Mind:*

The Seventeenth Century, p. 196). Harvard did indeed continue to teach ethics as a separate discipline in the curriculum, but neither Morison nor Miller observes the conspicuous disappearance of the class of ethical theses from the commencement broadsides after 1670. Two theses argued after 1670 directly support the position of Ames. Both of these were marked for actual disputation; the first was classified as a "physical thesis," while the second was classified as a "technological thesis." They read as follows: "There is no ethics distinct in species from theology" (1678, thesis 17) and "Ethics does not really differ from theology" (1687, thesis 12).

81. This treatise has been published in the original Latin with an English translation by H. W. Schneider in Herbert and Carol Schneider, eds., *Samuel Johnson: His Career and Writings* (New York: Columbia University Press, 1929), 2:55–186.

82. "Art is the idea representing and directing eupraxia. Idea is the matter of art. An idea is the model [*exemplar*] of a thing. The idea is to represent and by representing to direct eupraxia in acting. . . . The object and end of the idea is eupraxia" (*Technologia ceu Technometria,* theses 1–4, 6, in *Samuel Johnson,* 2:62).

83. The last thesis on theology reads as follows: "See about all these things Dr. W. Ames in *Marrow of Theology* and *Cases of Conscience*" (*Technologia ceu Technometria,* thesis 1,267, in *Samuel Johnson,* 2:182).

84. Ibid., 1,268–71, p. 184.

85. Ibid., p. 57.

86. Ibid., p. 186.

87. See Perry Miller, *Jonathan Edwards* (New York: World Publishing, 1963), pp. 57–58; see also H. W. Schneider, "Introduction: The Mind of Samuel Johnson," in *Samuel Johnson,* 2:186.

88. "Memoirs of the Life of the Rev. Dr. Johnson, and Several Things relating to the State both of Religion and Learning in his Times," in *Samuel Johnson,* 1:6.

89. See the charts outlining Johnson's classification of the academic system in *Samuel Johnson,* 2:368, 441.

90. For example, see Ames's approval of Bacon's work in *Technometry,* thesis 70, p. 105.

91. *Elementa Philosophica* (Philadelphia, 1752), pp. 3–4, 8–9.

In relation to this topic, see theses 18–63 of Johnson's *Technologia ceu Technometria* and the text of and commentary notes on theses 3, 15, and 44–48 of Ames's *Technometry*.

92. The precise relationship between Edwards and Johnson is problematic. The suggestion that Edwards might have learned of the philosophical idealism of Berkeley through Johnson is unlikely, for there is no evidence that Johnson himself knew of Berkeley's philosophy before he traveled to England in 1723. Furthermore, even though Johnson is often referred to as Edwards' "tutor," the contact between the two could only have been during a few weeks in 1716 and 1718. Johnson was not appointed tutor until 1716, and between the time of Edwards's matriculation and the beginning of his permanent residence in New Haven in June 1719 Edwards spent most of his time with an anti-Johnson student faction in Wethersfield. Johnson had been forced to resign in March 1719. Nevertheless, there is a reference in Edwards's "Catalogue" of books in his personal library to a book that had been recommended to him by Johnson, thereby indicating that there was at least some exchange between the two. Whatever the extent of the interaction between them, there remains the striking parallel in the education of both Johnson and Edwards in having been trained in the logic and method of Ramus and in Puritan technometry before they discovered the new logic and philosophy of Locke.

93. In a promising new line of investigation in Edwards studies, several scholars have argued that Edwards's reading of Locke must be set in the context of his previous training in logic, rhetoric, and metaphysics. William S. Morris has argued that the "old logic" in which Edwards was trained was not the logic of Peter Ramus but that of Franco Burgersdijck and Adrian Heereboord, who were Dutch Calvinist, Suaresian, Aristotelian, late scholastic logicians and metaphysicians; see "The Genius of Jonathan Edwards," in Jerald C. Brauer, ed., *Reinterpretation in American Church History,* (Chicago: University of Chicago Press, 1968), vol. 5, *Essays in Divinity,* pp. 29–30; see also his doctoral dissertation on "The Young Jonathan Edwards: A Reconstruction" (University of Chicago, 1955), pp. 31–32. On the other hand, another current Edwards scholar has argued that

the "old logic" is that of Ramus and the Aristotelian-scholastic syllogism, while the "new logic" is that of Port Royal written by Antoine Arnauld and Pierre Nicolet in *The Art of Thinking,* the popular medium through which Cartesian logic was spread abroad during the late seventeenth and early eighteenth centuries; see Leon Howard, *"The Mind" of Jonathan Edwards: A Reconstructed Text* (Berkeley: University of California Press, 1963), pp. 7–10, 122. Though one should not detract from the importance of the work of Morris and Howard, the problem of Edwards's logical studies is not as easily settled as these two scholars imply. As a matter of fact, both Burgersdijck and Heereboord were heavily influenced by Ramus's thought (Heereboord was also influenced by Cartesian thought) and are to be classified with Alsted and Keckermann as "systematics"; see Howell, *Logic and Rhetoric in England,* pp. 303, 309–11. We know from the Yale statutory provisions of Edwards's time that he spent a good part of his first two years studying logic. Moreover, in a description of the curriculum slightly before Edwards matriculated at Yale, it was clearly stated that the logic of Burgersdijck was read as soon as possible; see Oviatt, *The Beginnings of Yale,* p. 239. Another passage from a letter of a Yale graduate of 1714 sets the name of Ramus alongside those of Burgersdijck and Heereboord for the study of logic; see F. B. Dexter, *Biographical Sketches of the Graduates of Yale College, 1701–1745* (New York, 1885), p. 115. Edwards owned not only a 1634 edition of Ames's *Marrow of Theology* but also, and even more significantly, a copy of his summary of Ramist logic, *Theses Logicae;* see John D. Eusden, *The Marrow of Theology,* p. 2. The influence of Burgersdijck, and perhaps that of Heereboord, may also have been transmitted at least indirectly to Edwards through Charles Morton's *Compendium Logicae,* a volume that was included in Edwards's textbooks. With regard to the "Port Royal logic," Edwards wrote to his father on 19 July 1719 a letter in which he requested *The Art of Thinking;* this letter is quoted in Leon Howard, *"The Mind" of Jonathan Edwards,* pp. 4–7. The influence of Cartesian logic was probably also transmitted through William Brattle's *A Compendium of Logick* (1686), which was in use at both Harvard and Yale at the time. In short, Edwards's background reading and training in logic, like that of the rest of New Englanders in this period, was eclectic and synthetic. We shall not go far amiss if we conclude, therefore, that when Edwards speaks about the "old logic," he is referring to his training in the logic of traditional Aristotelian scholasticism, of Ramus, and of the "systematics" Burgersdijck and Heereboord, and perhaps of Keckermann and Alsted. When Edwards speaks of "other" or "new" logic, he is referring primarily to that of Locke and perhaps secondarily that of Port Royal.

94. "The Mind," Number 17, in *The Philosophy of Jonathan Edwards from his Private Notebooks,* ed. Harvey G. Townsend (Eugene, Ore.: University of Oregon Press, 1955), p. 33.

95. *The Philosophical Theology of Jonathan Edwards* (New York: Columbia University Press, 1960), pp. 29–30, 168.

96. For example, Schneider refers to Ramus as "a French humanist and Platonist who launched a vigorous attack on the logic and rhetoric of Aristotelian scholasticism" and goes on to say that Ramus's "chief philosophical contribution was to revive and systematize a Platonic dialectic or dichotomy as basic to and more useful than the scholastic and Aristotelian logic of demonstration" (*A History of American Philosophy*, p. 5). Although these statements are not inaccurate or misleading in themselves, they become so when not balanced by the Aristotelian components that continued to permeate Ramist thought.

97. See, for example, *The New England Mind: The Seventeenth Century,* p. 149.

98. Ong's substantial treatment of Ramism in *Ramus: Method and the Decay of Dialogue* is in many respects an Aristotelian sympathizer's continuation into the twentieth century of the bitter sixteenth- and seventeenth-century controversy between Ramists and Aristotelians. This critical judgment of Ong's work has been shared, although expressed differently, by Hugh Kearney, who recently wrote that Ong's work "exaggerates the importance of Ramism by placing it in an interpretation of history, popularized by Marshall McLuhan, in which Ramism is seen as a key to the Renaissance trend away from oral to visual culture" (*Scholars and Gentlemen,* p. 46).

99. "The Young Jonathan Edwards," p. 83; see also pp. 76, 795.

100. Ibid., p. 808.

101. Ibid., pp. 808–9.

102. Ibid., p. 92.

103. "He [Ames] wished to proscribe in theology, and in discussion of the Bible, as in philosophy, all metaphysical and (non-Christian) ethical notions" (Ibid., p. 81; see also p. 83).

104. *Jonathan Edwards,* p. 59.

105. Ibid., p. 54.

106. Ibid., pp. 54–55.

107. Ibid., p. 56.

108. Ibid., p. 58.

109. *The New England Mind: The Seventeenth Century,* p. 177.

110. Wallace E. Anderson has argued that it is more accurate to speak of Edwards as an "immaterialist" than as an "idealist"; see "Immaterialism in Jonathan Edwards' Early Philosophical Notes," *Journal of the History of Ideas* 25[1964]:181–200. I have chosen to speak more conventionally of Edwards's "idealism" in the sense of "the philosophical tendency to reduce all reality to states of mental consciousness."

111. The dating of these early manuscript notes is intimately bound up with discerning the time when Edwards studied Locke's *Essay Concerning Human Understanding* (1690). See the appendices to volume 1 of *The Works of President Edwards, with a Memoir of His Life,* ed. Sereno Dwight (New York, 1830). See also Egbert C. Smyth, "Some Early Writings of Jonathan Edwards," *Proceedings of the American Antiquarian Society,* n.s. 10(1896):222–23; Leon Howard, *"The Mind" of Jonathan Edwards; A Reconstructed Text,* p. 8; Wallace E. Anderson, "Mind and Nature in the Early Philosophical Writings of Jonathan Edwards," (Ph.D. diss., University of Minnesota, 1961, p. 36). Any final dating of these early manuscript notes, as well as a full study of Edwards's intellectual development, will be greatly expedited by Thomas A. Schafer's edition of the "Miscellanies" (the series of notes that Edwards began at Yale and to which he added throughout his life) and by Wallace E. Anderson's edition of "The Philosophical Writings," two forthcoming volumes in the Yale University Press edition of *The Works of Jonathan*

Edwards. In the meantime, the basic argument that Edwards's thought was influenced by certain idealist and empiricist strains in Puritan technometry is not affected by acknowledging the presently accepted boundaries of 1716 and 1726 for the writing of the early manuscript notes.

112. "The Mind," Number 27, in *The Philosophy of Jonathan Edwards from His Private Notebook,* ed. Harvey G. Townsend, p. 5.

113. "The Mind," number 10, ibid., p. 30.

114. "The Mind," number 34, ibid., p. 39.

115. "Of Being," ibid., p. 6.

116. "The Mind," number 13, ibid., p. 32.

117. I. Woodbridge Riley has an excellent survey of the older scholarship and literature on this problem in *American Philosophy: The Early Schools* (New York: Dodd, Mead, and Co., 1907), p. 129. Other important older discussions of the problem include the following: A. C. Fraser, *Life of Berkeley* (Oxford, 1871), pp. 182–90; Georges Lyon, *L' Idéalisme en Angleterre au XVIIIe Siécle* (Paris, 1888), chap. 10; Egbert C. Smyth, "Jonathan Edwards's Idealism," *The American Journal of Theology* 1(1897):950–64; Adam Leroy Jones, *Early American Philosophers* (New York, 1898), esp. pp. 8–9; H. N. Gardiner, "The Early Idealism of Jonathan Edwards," *Philosophical Review* 11(1902):26–42; Herbert W. Schneider, *A History of American Philosophy,* pp. 11–32; Ola Elizabeth Winslow, *Jonathan Edwards* (New York: Collier Books, 1961), pp. 64 ff. A useful recent summary of the older literature may be found in Douglas J. Elwood, *The Philosophical Theology of Jonathan Edwards,* pp. 169–70.

118. See Sereno E. Dwight, *The Works of President Edwards,* 1:64 ff.; see also Perry Miller, *Jonathan Edwards,* pp. 60, 62.

119. Without getting involved in the exaggerations and distortions related to the thesis that Edwards was a "hidden empiricist" or a "naturalist," the words "empiricist" and empiricism" are used here in the broad sense explicated by Perry Miller: "'History, observation, and experience are the things which must determine the question.' In these respects Edwards

must be called, as this study will call him, an empiricist. This is not to say, however, that Edwards held tentative hypotheses subject to constant alternation by further experiment. . . . Edwards went to nature and experience, not in search of the possible, but of the given, of that which cannot be controverted, of that to which reason has access only through perception and pain, that of which logic is the servant and from which dialectic receives its premises" (*Jonathan Edwards,* pp. 45–46).

120. "The Mind," number 13, in *The Philosophy of Jonathan Edwards from His Private Notebooks,* ed. Harvey G. Townsend, p. 32.

121. See "The Mind," number 34, ibid., p. 39.

122. The doctrine of "idea" as "repetition" is of crucial importance in distinguishing Edwards's empirical epistemology and idealist metaphysics both from Locke's doctrine of representation and from the more traditional Platonic doctrine of imitation or participation. For Edwards, human ideas of things do not simply represent or imitate things but actually repeat them over again; see "The Mind," number 66, ibid., p. 66.

123. "Miscellanies," number 782, ibid., p. 118.

124. Edwards describes in the following way what he means by calling God an intelligent agent: "For there is nothing whatsoever that we look upon as a sign or mark of intelligence in any being but it is in thus directing and ordering things for final causes. For we can see no signs of intelligence in any but these three, viz., 1. that he acts and produces effects. And 2. that, in acting or producing effects, he shows that things not present in their actual existence are yet some way present with him, as in idea, by a conformity of his acts to things distant or future. . . . And 3. that he acts with design, as aiming at that which is future" ("Miscellanies," number 749, ibid., p. 84).

125. *A Dissertation concerning the End for which God created the World,* in *The Works of Jonathan Edwards* (London, 1871), 2:97.

126. Ibid., p. 106.

127. Ibid., p. 101. cf. *Technometry,* thesis 60, p. 103, below.

128. *A Dissertation,* p. 119.

129. Edwards's most complete definition and description of true virtue are set forth in *The Nature of True Virtue,* in *The Works of Jonathan Edwards,* 1:127.

130. *A History of the Work of Redemption,* in *The Works of Jonathan Edwards,* 1:616.

131. "Reason shows, that it is fit and requisite that the intelligent and rational beings of the world should know something of God's scheme and design in his works: for they doubtless are principally concerned. God's great design in his works, is doubtless concerning his reasonable creatures, rather than brute beasts and lifeless things. . . . Further, it is fit that mankind should be somewhat informed of God's design in the government of the world, because they are made capable of actively falling in with that design, of promoting it, and acting herein as his friends and subjects" (ibid., p. 617).

132. *A Treatise Concerning Religious Affections,* in *The Works of Jonathan Edwards,* 1:314.

133. Ibid., pp. 325–26.

134. Ibid., pp. 322–23.

135. Robert K. Merton has pointed out the intimate connection of Protestantism and Puritanism to modern science and technology. The following quotation is a neat summary of the position set forth by Ames in his *Technometry:* "In every instance, the association of Protestantism with scientific and technologic interests and achievements is pronounced. . . . The association is largely understandable in terms of the norms embodied in both systems. The positive estimation by Protestants of a hardly disguised utilitarianism of intra-mundane interests, of a thorough-going empiricism, of the right and even the duty of *libre examen,* and of the explicit individual questioning of authority were congenial to the same values found in modern science. And perhaps above all is the significance of the active, ascetic drive which necessitated the study of Nature that it might be controlled. Hence, these two fields were well integrated and, in essentials, mutually supporting, not only in seventeenth-century England but in other times and places" (*Social Theory and Structure* [Glencoe, Ill.: Free Press, 1961], p. 595).

136. See, for example, Jacques Ellul, *The Technological Society,* trans. John Wilkinson (New York: Alfred A. Knopf, 1965).

137. See Max Lerner, "Big Technology and Neutral Technicians," in *The Dilemma of Organizational Society,* ed. Hendrik M. Ruitenbeck (New York: E. P. Dutton & Co., 1963), pp. 77–78.

138. Langdon Gilkey has clearly expressed this practical and "pragmatic" orientation of American theology and religion: "When creative theological formulations have appeared in America, as they surely have, they have been directed to 'doing' religion rather than to giving to religion systematic intellectual form. Dogmatic or ecclesiastical theology for its own sake has seldom been a characteristic of American theology. . . . Another way of describing this same characteristic is to point to the 'pragmatic' character of American religion and to the theological reflection stemming from it. If religion is an affair of the individual person, then its significance lies in what it does in the person's life— how it affects his character and behavior on the one hand, and his resultant attitudes toward life on the other. American theology has avoided purely theoretical issues and problems; its energies have been directed toward results, and these primarily in the ethical field. The creative theologians in America . . . have generally been ethicists" ("Social and Intellectual Sources of Contemporary Protestant Theology in America," *Daedalus* [Winter 1967], pp. 78–79). H. Richard Niebuhr has also pointed to roots of the pragmatic character of American Protestantism in the sense of orientation in a divinely governed world: "The pragmatism, the experimentalism, and the changefulness of order in Protestantism, perhaps particularly in America, may be due in considerable part to this sense of orientation in a dynamic, divinely governed world" ("The Protestant Movement and Democracy in the United States," in *The Shaping of American Religion,* ed. James W. Smith and A. Leland Jamison [Princeton, N.J.: Princeton University Press, 1961], p. 47).

139. Nethenus, *Ames,* pp. 20–21.

WILLIAM AMES | TECHNOMETRY

Technometry,

which adequately circumscribes the Boundaries and the Ends of all the Arts and of every individual Art

Thesis 1. Art is the idea of εὐπραξία, *eupraxia* or good action, methodically delineated by universal rules.

2. Although the word "art" may be τῶν μέσων, ambiguous, and may signify various things in various parts, it is nevertheless clear in what part and in what significance it is taken by us.

3. It is not a Platonic idea existing in some particular corner of the world but rather a model (*exemplar*), such as Plautus looks toward, or the delineation or the form of a model formed in the mind of an artificer before action and for the sake of action, so that it may represent and, by representing, rule the action.

4. Every agent not acting by chance acts first because of a form, for there could be no action unless he should have a form pre-existing within himself through a likeness. Surely an agent acts as from art, either according to natural being (if he be acting naturally) or according to intelligible being (if he be acting from counsel). And that likeness of the form is called an idea, just as the likeness of a house preexisting in the mind of an architect is called the idea of a house.

5. Art is an idea rather than a habit, a teaching, a discipline, a faculty, a book, a system, or a virtue. For "idea," comprehending all those things that are more truly said about art and being in general appropriate to every art, expresses most properly and most closely the general essence of art.

6. Of course, art can also be called a habit, either because it is possessed (*habetur*) or because it makes the one possessing it apt for (*habentem se habilem*) and capable of working. This is why the German word *Kunst,* "art," being derived from *können,* "to be able," takes right aim. But neither of the above concepts constitutes the essence of art; rather, each one follows after art has been constituted, the former as an adjunct and the latter as an effect. Therefore, "habit" less fittingly defines the genus of art.

7. Art can also be called a teaching (*doctrina*) insofar as it is taught; a discipline insofar as it is learned; a faculty insofar as it facilitates acting; a book or a system insofar as it is formed by pen or type in many letters composed among themselves and once inscribed in a book or on bark. These, however, are not primarily of the essence of art but either precede the constituting of it in and for men or follow after it has been constituted.

8. Art cannot be called a virtue, except insofar as the teaching of virtue is a part of an individual art, or insofar as the science of any thing is called "virtue" by the Greeks because this science leads in no small way to exercising more rightly virtuous action. This is why the arts are also commonly called "intellectual virtues." These origins may perhaps be a sufficient reason for those who deduce the word "art" either from ἀρετή, virtue, or from ארה, he was strong, from which they deduce the word ἀρετή itself. Nevertheless, virtue can hardly be for us the reason of the genus or the general essence of art.

9. Art is the idea of eupraxia, having eupraxia not only as the object that the idea is concerned with representing but also as the end toward which the idea tends to direct by representing.

10. It is held by others that mind and will are the object of art, and that the guidance or direction of both mind and will is the end of art. But they speak less accurately when they go on to say that the mind is directed in cognition and that the will is directed in action. For here it is clear that cognition and action are directed principally and objectively, but the mind and the will are directed

only subjectively insofar as cognition and action are rooted in them.

11. We do not deny the last statement above; rather, we further concede that the mind and the will, insofar as they are directed by art, are the subject of art, insofar as the operations of art are grounded in them.

12. But guidance and direction are not so much the end of art as part of its general essence, namely, of the idea absolutely constituted in representing and ruling.

13. Eupraxia is the regular motion (*motus*) of an agent in acting.

14. Art conveys with itself an aptitude for this eupraxia to all those into whom it enters. Even if the use of this aptitude is not so perfect in men—not only because of the imperfection of the arts in them but also because of the weakness of the human powers required for acting—nevertheless, eupraxia does not on that account cease to be the end of art.

15. Although this eupraxia (both as the idea of art and as art itself), insofar as it exists in God or the exercise of God, is one unique and most simple act; nevertheless, in the work exercised (namely, in created things that are all concrete and divisible), it comes out manifold and various as it were from a refraction of rays,* and therefore is perceived by the eye of reason and exercised by man as manifold and divided.

16. Eupraxia is divided, I say, first into genesis and analysis as the parts generally integrating it and vitally expressing the reciprocation of its motion.

17. For genesis is the regular procession from simples to composites, the latter being constituted from the former.

18. Analysis is the regular regression from composites to simples, the former being resolved into the latter.

19. This motion in eupraxia, whether it be progression (i.e.,

---

* The 1633 London edition reads "from a refraction of reason." The 1651 edition of the *Technometria* and *Alia Technometriae Delineatio* both read "from a refraction of rays."

genesis) or regression (i.e., analysis), is therefore so strictly reciprocal that regularly (1) wherever one of them ceases or begins,
there the other begins or ceases, and (2) each one follows the
other's footsteps.

20. That genesis which follows after analysis is called by the
particular name "imitation," which, with respect to its general
nature, properly belongs in this and not in another place (*locus*).

21. In the same manner genesis and analysis in general cannot
be taught elsewhere than here in connection with art in general,
since any individual art, as it pursues the teaching of special
analysis and genesis, is thus ordered with its beginning [in that
special analysis and genesis].

22. Secondly, eupraxia is divided into general and special. We
do not say that eupraxia is divided into genus and species, as if
one were the genus or species of the other; for general, as much
as special, is a species of eupraxia as of a common genus. But
general eupraxia is distinct with respect to the use that it has in
all other eupraxiae and in itself. This is why we say that general
eupraxia becomes concrete in all other eupraxiae and in itself.
Special eupraxia is distinct because its use is more special and
thus does not extend itself widely.

23. General eupraxia is Cicero's "discoursing well" ($\varepsilon\vec{v}\delta\iota\alpha\lambda\acute{\varepsilon}\gamma\varepsilon$-
$\sigma\theta\alpha\iota$, *bene disserere*), that is, disposing well the reasons of things
that have been invented well.

24. General eupraxia becomes concrete in use in all other
eupraxiae and in itself, and this from absolute necessity so that the
remaining eupraxiae cannot be known, or exist, or be exercised
without it. Hence, it is rightly called "universal" ($\kappa\alpha\theta o\lambda\iota\kappa\omega\tau\acute{\alpha}\tau\eta$).

25. In addition to this, there may legitimately be two other
general eupraxiae, namely, speaking (*loqui*) and communicating
(*dicere*). The image of the former general eupraxia, after it has
been received, brings forth these two other general eupraxiae by,
in, and for man. Nevertheless, since these two latter general
eupraxiae become concrete in the remaining eupraxiae only by
hypothetical necessity (namely, insofar as those things known by

someone are to be communicated to others), they cannot contend with the former in that generality of use.

26. And thus, a subdivision can be established whereby general eupraxia may be called more or less general: more as discoursing, less as speaking and communicating. Nonetheless, the difference that ought to be and customarily is observed between a mistress and her maidservant should be observed on both sides; for the two latter general eupraxiae are subject and serve as handmaidens to the former in consequence of its better being (*esse*)—at least in men.

27. Special eupraxia either becomes concrete in use in part only in some other eupraxia or it clearly does not. Therefore, it can be divided into less and more special.

28. Less special eupraxia is measuring well; more special eupraxia is doing the work of nature well or living well.

29. These eupraxiae are called special because they do not become concrete in use in all the other eupraxiae. This differentiates them from those eupraxiae that do and are therefore called general.

30. But one of these special eupraxiae is called less such, that is, less special, namely, to measure well. Measuring well is less special because it becomes concrete in part (that is to say, with respect to the dimensions of bodies) in another eupraxia, namely, doing the work of nature well. Doing the work of nature well and living well are more special because they do not become concrete in any part in any other eupraxia.

31. Perhaps some, unmindful of what has been said above, will judge that doing the work of nature is not the eupraxia of an art because it exceeds human powers. To these it must be repeatedly asserted that they will not sustain that the act of doing the work of nature utterly withdraws from man; for the works produced by the imitation of nature (*operibus per imitationem naturatis*), namely, the works of farmers, gardeners, workers, and many others, contradict them loudly. In man this act of doing the work of nature has been united with so much imper-

fection as can hardly be found in any other eupraxia—except perhaps in living well—and it has been observed that this is so both because the art of doing the work of nature has to this point been the most imperfect of all the arts in men, and also because the powers required to exercise that act have been greatly lacking in men.

32. Since something made by motion (or some *thing* [*res*], as the logicians say, made by motion), necessarily and immediately follows every motion, the thing or εὐπραττόμενον, *euprattomenon* or good work, made by the motion of art or any kind of eupraxia must follow.

33. This is why, according to the mind of Aristotle, every discipline will be an art—because every discipline is ἕξις μετὰ λογόυ ποιητική, a habit capable of making according to reason and leaving a work after itself. For, as a reminder, the eupraxiae of the individual disciplines have their own euprattomena. This can also be easily rendered manifest by induction. Discoursing, or the discipline of discoursing, leaves after itself invented and disposed arguments; speaking leaves fitting speech; communicating leaves embellished speech; measuring leaves measured things; doing the work of nature leaves natures; living leaves life.

34. Those who want the work left by art to be external and perceptible to the senses should first truly demonstrate, before they will persuade us, that ποίησις, making, means only this, and thus reconcile their master Aristotle with themselves. This may not be done by quoting certain passages of Aristotle where it is said that a work of art is perceptible to the senses, for we do not deny that the works of some or indeed many of our arts are perceptible to the senses. But it does not follow at all from this that every work of every art ought to be perceptible to the senses, or that ποίησις, making, signifies only work perceptible to the senses.

35. Although the euprattomena, like the eupraxiae and their precepts, are distinct among themselves and from each other, nevertheless their use, as that which joins them together and in which a posterior art and the precept of a posterior art always use

the work of a prior art, is common and confused. Thus, in this example: "By the same measure by which you measure, it will be measured to you," the use of the distinct prattomena of logic, grammar, rhetoric, mathematics, and theology is common and confused. So it is in the following: "New wine must not be put into old wine skins," where beyond the previous prattomena there is also the use of the prattomenon of physics.

36. But just as prattomena are confused in use, so they are abstracted and separated by speculation. By this means, any prattomenon whatever is allotted to its own discipline. Since this is the consequent that is about to come into being in the delineation of the arts, we may fix our attention upon this delineation.

37. The idea of eupraxia is delineated not by one but by many delineations. The singular eupraxiae are conceived as absolute by God (as explained above) and are extricated by man not by one but by many acts.

38. These delineations, because they represent their eupraxia faithfully and without any deceit, are called ἀξιώματα, axioms worthy of faith; because they rule the following eupraxia, they are called rules; because they rule by commanding, like the edicts of magistrates, they are called precepts; because judgment and examination of both acts and actors are regulated according to them, they are called κριτήρια, criteria, or canons; because the projected prattomena are seen and appear in them, they are called problems (*problemata*), theorems (*theoremata*), phenomena (φαινόμενα).

39. We have preferred to call these delineations rules, since "rule" is of the primary essence of "idea" and best expresses the best known force of art.

40. But these rules, since they have been and are at first in the most true, most just, and most wise God, must be most true, most just, and most wise (i.e., in a word, "universal").

41. Since these rules ought to rule* certainly and infallibly—this is why those are right who want "art" to have been derived

---

* "To rule" has been inserted on the basis of the reading in *Alia Technometriae Delineatio,* thesis 47, p. 56.

from *arx,* tower, because art, like a fortified tower, excludes (*arceat*) all errors from eupraxia—they cannot be true only in part (that is, doubtful), much less can they be by any reason unjust or unwise. Hence, we have said that this idea is delineated by universal rules.

42. The rules will be most true if their principles are harmonious with the law of truth, κατὰ παντὸς, that is, if their principles are of such a kind that when they are axiomatically composed among themselves, the consequent is true about the whole antecedent. Those principles that do not enunciate a consequent about the whole antecedent are, because of the diversity of the assumed antecedent, as much false as true, and by and in themselves are neither true nor false.

43. Understanding (*intelligentia*) is the invention* of these principles, which are nothing other than those individual aspects of individual things. For we have been accustomed to call him "understanding" who perceives individually that which is in individual things.

44. In God this understanding is archetypal, in man it is ectypal.

45. Since this understanding is in God immediately from eternity, by no means being conveyed to Him or impressed upon Him, it is truly in him ἀρχὴ τοῦ τυποῦ καὶ παντὸς καὶ πρώτου, the principle both of every type (*typus*) and of the first type. But this understanding expresses itself as if it were through a certain refraction in created and governed things that are our understanding's type, from which human understanding is gathered.

46. This is why this understanding is called "theology," but taken as a whole it must be called "art"; insofar as it exists in God, it must be called "archetypal," because it is nothing other than God's eternal wisdom, the creator and governor of things.

47. Man's art also has to do with certain things, and thus it is the cause and principle of some type by imitation. Nevertheless, since it is not the principle either of the first or of every type,

---

* "The invention" has been inserted on the basis of the reading in *Alia Technometriae Delineatio,* thesis 50, p. 57.

as is God's understanding or art (for any human art has taken some other type for a principle), man's art is called ectypal rather than archetypal.

48. Type (namely, that in which all art shines and from which its principles, which produce human understanding, are gathered by man) is primarily things created and governed by God but secondarily things made or conceived in a similar manner by man.

49. Hence, the Greeks call art τέχνη from τεύχομαι, I make or frame (*fabrico*), obviously because art is impressed upon the fabric of a thing from which it shines as from its type.

50. These things, insofar as they exist, are called "being" (*Ens*), that is, if you lay the word open, "that which is" (*quod est*); insofar as they are conceived to be, they are either possible ("being possible of being conceived," *Ens fictum possibile*) or impossible ("being impossible of being conceived," *Ens fictum impossibile*). Yet that which is conceived to be may also be called "non-being" (*Non-Ens*) insofar as it truly is not, and "the being of pure reason or of the one reasoning" (*Ens rationis purae, aut ratiocinantis*) insofar as it is and exists in reason alone or in the understanding of someone. Likewise, on the other hand, something that is not is called "non-being" (*Non-Ens*): if it is not so that it clearly opposes being, it is called "negative non-being" (*Non-Ens negativum*); if it is not so that it can sometimes be, it is called "potential non-being" or "potential being" (*Non-Ens potentiale aut Ens potentiale*); if it is not so that it ought to have been, it is called "privative non-being" (*Non-Ens privativum*).

51. We certainly owe no praise to metaphysics in the naming of these or any other appellations that are seen to have been imposed upon things insofar as they are. Yet we do owe metaphysics some censure because it has put its sickle into a harvest not its own and because it has unjustly claimed for itself that which is proper to etymological lexicons—unless perhaps it wishes to be taken for a logical (or a general philosophical) but most imperfect lexicon.

52. But if metaphysics should contend that these or other

similar appellations are owed to itself not as appellations but with respect to their reasons, it surely falls upon Scylla. For then logic, from which alone the reasons for these and any other general appellations of being are taken, will justly bring action against it.

53. For when I know or say that a thing or some being is one, true, good, perfect, before, after, at the same time, universal, singular, cause, effect, possible, necessary, contingent, easy, difficult, adorned with duration and place, a measure or measured, the same with any other mode, diverse, related, apparent, complex, opposite—this is only through the logical precepts of invention and disposition. These precepts teach one to know these and similar affections of things, although several (or at least not all) of these words may not be comprehended in logic.

54. That discipline whose task it is to transmit the whole nature of things, namely, physics, shows whether any being has a nature either subsisting by itself (*per se*) or inhering in some other (that is, whether any being is a substance or an accident)— as will be easy for anyone to see with what we have previously set forth from the resolution of being insofar as it is the type of art, with which we shall deal immediately.

55. This type, which we have said is things themselves or being itself, has taken form from all the arts' principles, which not only appear and shine forth around the type but also in it.

56. Reason, relation, and the mutual affection of things shine forth around the type from all sides and from its every part, so that by this means the things themselves are conveyed to our understanding, which does not perceive otherwise than under reason and some affection. Hence the principles of discoursing.

57. With and in this reason, relation, and mutual affection of things, the appellations of things or words (namely, those things that are taken from the reason or some affection of a thing) are also radically comprehended. Therefore, by these mediating appellations or words, things are conveyed from man to man. Hence the principles of speaking and communicating.

58. First, quantity is seen in the type, for all things are pri-

marily made from matter (so that they thus immediately differ at the first from God) and are therefore quantities. Hence the principles of measuring.

59. Secondly, natures are seen in the type, for things are secondarily distinct from each other especially through form, which is the particular nature of things.

60. Thirdly, the end is seen in the type. The end is that universal goodness (namely, the glory of God) which is seen in all things and toward which all things look, like some arrow shot in a straight line. Plato has understood this: "He never practices anything either moral or dialectical, either mathematical or physical, but that he may soon withdraw with the greatest piety to the contemplation and worship of God" (M. Ficino, Preface, *Platonic Theology*).* Hence the principles of living.

61. In the beginning the type of created things was most perfectly rendering all these things [mentioned in theses 56–60] easily accessible to man, who was still established in the state of integrity. But since man has fallen, the goodness not only of the remaining creatures (which have been subjected to a curse and vanity because of man) but also of man himself (in whose conscience goodness had especially shone) has been so obscure and darkened that its principles remain to be comprehended there by us only as very few and indeed very corrupted.

62. Nevertheless, God also mercifully and wisely resolved this for us when he substituted the Scriptures for the type deficient in that part of things [that is, in the goodness of things]. In the Scriptures he has most perfectly revealed the principles of goodness, that is, the principles of honesty, piety, justice, and equity.

63. Hence, being thoughtless or ungrateful and yet not impious by law, do they listen who—educated in the bosom of the Church, have thoroughly learned both about the obscurity of these principles in the type of things, which furthermore each one (alas!) perceives well enough by and in himself, and about the new

*Marsilio Ficino, *Prooemium in Platonicam Theologiam,* in *Opera Omnia* (Turin: Bottega d'Erasmo, 1962), 1:78.

revelation in the Scriptures—yet flee from these Scriptures to search after the principles of what they call "practical philosophy" and of law and seduce others with themselves.

64. The very pagans (whom the persons above prefer in part to Holy Scripture) tacitly approve by their example what I have said above. For it was certainly not shameful for them to seek the truer principles of goodness, which they perceived to be absent from their natures, not only directly but also indirectly from the writings of the Hebrews who were either living among them or elsewhere. This has been set forth in the histories.

65. This is why so many praiseworthy vestiges of honesty appear in their writings; therefore, we clearly do not wish these writings to be removed from the hands of all, even though they should be subordinated to and tested according to the Holy Scriptures. Furthermore, they should not be taken as the rule and canon of life or of morals and law while Holy Scripture has been neglected.

66. With the exception of goodness, the type of things still conveys perfectly enough the remaining principles; but these remaining principles are to be inwardly seen and gathered only by those penetrating by untiring analysis the inner aspects of type.

67. No one will have inwardly known and clearly perceived the principles of goodness revealed in the Holy Scriptures unless, after careful analysis of these Scriptures has been made, the eyes of his mind have been opened at the same time by the Holy Spirit. The latter [i.e., the opening of the eyes of the mind by the Holy Spirit] is completely and absolutely necessary, but with respect to the former [i. e., the careful analysis of the Scriptures], it is certainly very useful to investigate the remaining principles.

68. Analysis of Holy Scripture is accomplished by the precepts of logic rightly applied.

69. Analysis of things begins αἰσθήσει, in sense perception. All things are either in themselves or by reason of their effects φαινόμενα and αἰσθητὰ, that is, appearances or perceptibles without apprehending the intervention of another. Analysis is carried

forward ἱστορίᾳ, by observation, which carefully notes and retains those things that have been perceived by sense perception and their incipient cognition. Analysis is completed ἐπαγωγῇ, by induction, which seriously compares with each other those things that have often been perceived by sense and retained by observation, and which concludes what of certainty follows. Analysis is confirmed ἐμπειρίᾳ, by experience, which considers and reconsiders long and fully those things that have been concluded, and which accurately and strictly tests those things that have been given on any occasion.

70. To this point belong the investigations (*historiae*) of the individual arts, i. e., the notational or observational investigations as much as the inductive (which are called experiments or experimental). Lord Verulam depicts in his *Novum Organum* the mode of how these investigations ought to be woven together, and not only he but also Pliny and Aristotle in the *Historia Animalium,* have left behind a model (*exemplar*). This model is certainly of the greatest use not only for constituting the disciplines more truly but also for understanding and correcting them more easily—unless the dictatorial power of Aristotle and that excessive credulity in him should prevail to so great an extent.

71. From these things it is now easy to judge, first, what in the individual disciplines is the primary and principal fountain of errors, defects, and controversies (which are never to be ended by the literary studies that remain in that state): It is certainly the very great neglect of those things discussed above, which are necessary for gathering the most true principles.

72. And the greater this neglect is in physics, the more the fountain flows with faults, so that scarcely any of its matter is free from them. This is so because its numerous mystagogues not only do not themselves make experiments of natural things (from which they might either gather its truer principles, or test and correct those principles that have been gathered) but also rest so superstitiously in the scarcely accurate writings of

certain ancients that they believe themselves about to commit a sacrilege by departing from them, seeking first who has spoken rather than what he has said—even though the manifest truth that has been searched out and examined by others by reason of such experiments may convincingly advocate that they should so depart.

73. From these things it becomes clear, secondly, although respect and honor are owed to the ancients' writings of this kind, just how much respect and honor are owed. Other things being equal, the writings of more recent men should certainly be placed before, not after, the writings of the ancients. For several eyes may see better than one; one day may teach another; and second thoughts may be better than first thoughts.

74. From these things it becomes clear, thirdly, although honor is owed to the writings of pagans, just how much honor is owed. Other things being equal, the writings of Christians should certainly be placed before, not after, the writings of pagans. This is more fitting since the eyes of Christians have been more opened by divine grace.

75. From these things appears, fourthly, a distinction that must be made among Christian writers: That is to say, works brought forth by an incurable passion for scribbling and self-love are not to be regarded so highly as those accomplished from a sincere love of truth by the friends of God demonstrating themselves in uprightness of life.

76. From these things it is easy to judge, fifthly, that in theology and jurisprudence—if it be permissable to adhere to the opinions of any in an extremely obscure matter—the opinions of Christians are to be adhered to rather than those of the impious, even when very many.

77. Thus, let us not become the slaves of anyone, but, performing military service under the banner of free truth, let us freely and courageously follow the truth that leads and calls away from the hallucinations of our elders, as they are men who have also been created in the image of Adam. Testing all things,

retaining that which is good, let Plato be a friend, let Aristotle be a friend, but even more let truth (*veritas*) be a friend.

78. The most true principles, if they be composed according to the law of justice, κατὰ τὸ αὐτὸ, homogeneously or essentially, become most just rules. For wherever its own is given to anything, there it is done most justly.

79. Science (*scientia*) is judgment* of these principles that have been so composed. Primary and most true science is to know the causes and essences of things. This science is not only required in the one composing before the composition but also rises from the composition into those who truly comprehend the composition.

80. Such principles so composed, if they be distributed according to the law of wisdom, καθόλου πρῶτον, adequately and reciprocally, finally become the wisest rules. For those things that are extended neither more widely nor more narrowly than is just are deservedly said to be extended most wisely. Hence their wisdom.

81. This is the use of these laws in all the disciplines and in the individual disciplines with respect to all essential precepts and individual essential precepts. And unless these precepts be consistent with these laws, they are defective by law.

82. Now with respect to dwelling on important points (*commorationes*), they are in part exempted from these laws; but only very few are to be admitted, and only from just causes.

83. Others exempt canons and rules, and they contend that only definitions and divisions are to be measured according to these laws. But—lest I repeat what has been said—if they would only consider the appellation and end of "canon" or "rule," they will have to yield. How will that which is in some way crooked merit the name "right rule" or even κατ' ἐξοχὴν, *par excellence?* Or how could I test the absolute rectitude of any thing according to that which is such?

---

*Judgment" has been inserted on the basis of the reading in *Alia Technometriae Delineatio,* thesis 67, p. 63.

84. Finally, if this idea, standing in agreement with universal rules, be delineated methodically according to the law of prudence or method, prudence (*prudentia*) rises up from this. This prudence, joined to understanding, science, and wisdom, renders art complete.

85. These are the genuine nature and spring of those commonly so-called "habits" of the mind,* so that (as has become evident from what has been said) they are thus necessarily gathered in every art. Therefore, should any of these be lacking, the idea itself is lacking and may not arrive at the just completion of art.

86. Those perceiving this matter to be different and for the most part irrelevant, although they are ignorant, nevertheless produce justly and with support from all those ideas and disciplines that they altogether deny to be arts.

87. But those who withdraw science, or wisdom, or prudence from any discipline to that extent deprive that discipline of its merit, so that they tacitly or by interpretation say that its precepts are heterogeneous, or inadequate, or without method.

88. Thus far we have considered the nature and essence of art; its division now follows. The commonly accepted division of art into theoretical and practical is defective in many ways and therefore must be rejected.

89. This division is without any true difference, so that one of its members necessarily includes the other. For there is no contemplation that should not be practice and have its own work; nor is there any action in general such as to exclude all contemplation.

90. There is utterly no theoretical art that should not have its practice toward which (not resting in theory) it will tend from its nature. Nor is there any practical art that should be learned without theory, or in the theory of which its hearer, after he has

---

*"Of the mind" has been inserted on the basis of the reading in *Alia Technometriae Delineatio,* thesis 71, p. 64.

thoroughly learned it, is not able to rest, if he wishes, and often has so rested.

91. Concerning mathematics, it is acknowledged that it is practical enough.* Concerning metaphysics, we have also sometimes had adversaries publicly acknowledging that metaphysics has its practice.* Notwithstanding, it has been without practice concerning its most principal part, namely, the teaching that concerns God. Thus, it must certainly be concluded that metaphysics is vain and useless—indeed of such a kind as that which in the apostle's witness (Romans 1:21) is most severely punished by God—unless it be directed to practice. Finally, it has been stated before how the works of many bear witness concerning the practice of physics.

92. From these things it follows that, after all these things have been well considered, there may properly be for them no "practical" part of philosophy. For any precept of universal truth that is found in ethics, household economy, or politics properly looks toward theology. Nevertheless, they wish theology to be removed far away from their philosophy (so divided) or from their arts. Several things will be said about this in that which follows.

93. At the same time that fictitious interpretation of the word $\pi\rho\hat{\alpha}\xi\iota\varsigma$, practice, is taken for "virtuous action," and, having been reduced to extremities, they always try to escape by means of this fictitious interpretation. Although there is certainly no virtuous action that theology should not teach, either virtuous action or its likeness may ultimately be observed in or outside the Church in any subject whatever.

94. Any judicious person will perceive that those are deservedly accused who have wished to excuse themselves at this point by the example and authority of pagans. Since those in darkness,

---

*"That it is practical enough" and "that metaphysics has its practice" has been inserted on the basis of the reading in *Alia Technometriae Delineatio,* thesis 75, p. 65.

turning to the sparks of honesty found in themselves or drawn from another place, have variously intermingled various teachings, this division of art into theoretical and practical* can be ascribed to the defect not of those who have been taught more rightly from the Scriptures (with the Holy Spirit cooperating) but rather to their imitators.

95. Therefore, another truer division is to be substituted, a division that can be such that by means of it art is at one time called "general," at another time "special."

96. For since art's object, principles, and end are general or special (as is obvious from those things that have been said), the one who has known that art must be divided from its object, principles, and end will not doubt that art itself is general or special. That which has been foreshadowed here must be undertaken again in the following subdivisions.

97. Once more, general art is either primary or secondary (that is, either more general or less general).

98. The primary or more general art is dialectic, so called from its end, διαλέγεθαι, to discourse, namely, because it adequately transmits the invention and the dispositions of reasons that have been laid hold of concisely. Dialectic has indeed been taught genuinely and from its own nature by categories, but only by those categories with which equal, individual arguments are clothed. Dialectic utterly rejects any appendage of fallacies.

99. The secondary and less general arts are grammar and rhetoric.

100. Grammar is derived by synecdoche from γράφω, I write, for we have been accustomed to use the written word as much as the uttered word to express the perceptions of the mind.

101. Grammar is to transmit in the vernacular idiom of any people the Latin language, which is the first of foreign languages to be learned. But grammar is to translate the other languages into the Latin tongue, special and extraordinary things only

*"Division of art into theoretical and practical" has been inserted on the basis of the reading in *Alia Technometriae Delineatio,* thesis 77, p. 66.

having been changed; for that variety of method and of common definitions in the individual languages delays many people for a long time.

102. The precepts of grammar, because they must be adapted to languages (as its subject), which abound with many irregularities, and because it [grammar] is likewise, along with its associate [rhetoric], merely a handmaiden, to this extent cannot be transmitted as regular or as accommodated to the laws of the remaining arts.

103. Rhetoric is from ῥέω, I flow, which I say is from ἐρέω, I say (*dico*). In rhetoric the precepts of invention and of disposition are repeated heterogeneously.

104. These three arts are called general; and dialectic is more general, while grammar and rhetoric are less general because of the reasons applied in their acts, which have been spoken about above. Since these three arts become concrete in the remaining arts, these remaining arts cannot be known without the art and act of discoursing; cannot be spoken without the act and art of speaking; and cannot be communicated appropriately without the art and act of communicating.

105. The remaining three arts are mathematics, physics, and theology. These obviously have no use in the preceding arts, nor do they become concrete in them. Hence, they are "more special."

106. Mathematics is from μανθάνω, I learn, because boys once learned this art before the remaining arts to explore their natural talent and ability.

107. They commonly set up one abstract part and another concrete part of mathematics. But for all those who have considered the matter carefully, there is no concrete part of mathematics. Anything that is customarily transmitted in this concrete part belongs either to the art of physics or obviously to no art, but rather to the use and faculty of the art of mathematics or of the art of physics. We shall consider the use and faculty of these arts later.

108. In geometry, however, the principles of many of those

things that are said to pertain to concrete mathematics are to be transmitted; useless demonstrations are to be cut off; and practice is principally to be looked toward.

109. Physics is from φύσις, nature. Physics ought to comprehend and pursue the whole nature of all natural being, in genus as much as in species, and thus also of Spirits themselves (so far as it is universally capable).

110. Theology is ἀπὸ τῶν λόγων τοῦ θεοῦ, from the declarations (*eloquiis*) of God. By reason of its principles, theology is gathered from these declarations one by one; and therefore theology is defined by "teaching" (*doctrina*) rather than by "art."

111. Theology alone homogeneously transmits (1) the universal teaching about God, not as he is in himself (for he is not known in this manner by anyone except himself) but as he has revealed himself to us more clearly in the book of Scripture and more obscurely in the book of nature so that we might live well.

112. But there are those who make a distinction of the teaching about God, insofar as he can be known either by natural or by supernatural light, and they want that teaching only insofar as it is known by supernatural light to pertain to theology. These people have been abundantly refuted in the seventh thesis of *Against Metaphysics,* by these reasons in summary. First, because a real difference of knowledge cannot be the mode or respect of reason in an object; rather, a real difference must necessarily be something real, as Scotus has testified in the *Prologue to the Distinctions.* Secondly, because the level of knowledge that is denoted by "insofar as he can be known by natural light, etc." can no more constitute a diverse species of teaching than "insofar as something can be known by an uneducated man, by a boy, or by one not sufficiently sound in mind." Thirdly, nothing can be known about God by natural light except either through effects or through argumentation from one attribute to another; and this also may come into being by supernatural light. Fourthly, revelation or natural light is indeed the efficient cause of theology but not the formal reason specifying and distinguish-

ing it from the other disciplines. Fifthly, anything of truth and certainty that is known about God by natural light has likewise been divinely revealed; that is, it is known by supernatural light. Therefore, if anything of truth and certainty that is known about God be dealt with separately a second time, teachings are multiplied at least without necessity.

113. Theology alone homogeneously transmits (2) the universal teaching of virtues (i.e., of honesty, law, and equity). Theology alone homogeneously delivers the whole revealed will of God for directing our morals, will, and life. This whole revealed will of God alone is that right reason—if absolute rectitude be looked toward, as it must be looked toward here—in which alone, by the consensus of all who are of sound mind, the norm or rule of honesty, law, and equity (and therefore of virtues) is constituted.

114. Therefore, although there may be some usefulness and necessity of household economy and politics for jurisprudence, the principal usefulness and necessity is nevertheless theology's. Theology abundantly supplies most distinctly and most perfectly the general rules, the first principles, and all the foundations of law; household economy and politics convey to jurisprudence only some general rules and first principles that have been accommodated to their own uses.

115. There is clearly no usefulness and necessity of ethics for jurisprudence. For ethics may properly contain nothing except imperfection, while all the remaining things have been borrowed from theology.

116. Notwithstanding, the pretexts of the ethicists have thus now been often rewoven. The principal pretexts of the ethicists are as follows. (1) *They distinguish civil and moral happiness from supernatural and eternal happiness.* Nevertheless, (a) supernatural and eternal happiness, considered with respect to the civil and political society in which we live, is civil and moral. (b) That which they call civil and moral (in contradistinction to that which is supernatural) ought not deservedly to be called "natural," that is, that which proceeds from corrupted nature, but

rather "above nature," flowing from those vestiges of the integral state that remain through divine grace and have also been established and increased in a certain manner in the wiser pagans. (c) The proper good, the happiness or end of man, is not manifold. (d) That is not true virtue that may not lead man to his end and highest good. (2) *They say that the object of theology is the inner man and piety, while the object of ethics is external morals and uprightness (probitatem).* Nevertheless, external morals and uprightness are equally the object of theology, which commands external as much as internal obedience, as Keckermann also acknowledges in canon 10, "Concerning the End of Ethics," in *General Precognitions of the System of Ethics.* Ethics, no less than theology, claims for itself, the reform of man according to the image of God by prescribing the precepts of virtues and by calling away from vices. This is why prudence does not refuse to hear of ruling the will and appetite. (3) *They add that ethical virtues are confined to the limits of this life, while theological virtues are extended to the future life.* But first, if something should therefore immediately cease to be theological because it is confined to the limits of this life, many things that are truly theological would cease to be theological, such as the preaching of the Word, the administration of the sacraments, etc. Secondly, they will never be able to prove that any virtue in its essence is about to cease with this life, although in some particular individuals the likenesses of certain virtues may be about to cease. (4) *They say that the subject of ethics is the upright, good, and honest man; while the subject of theology is the religious and pious man.* That which has been said with respect to the second reason above applies here also. And they respond otherwise with respect to the first part of this assertion when they affirm that ethics teaches to live piously. With respect to the latter part of this assertion, according to Titus 2:12, Paul manifestly says that theology also teaches to live temperately and justly, that is, uprightly and honestly. (5) *The difference between ethical and theological virtues is excellently set forth first in Matthew 5:20 and also in chapters 6 and 7.* Nothing appears in these texts except that, for the sake of virtue, no one ought to propose for himself private usefulness and glory but honesty alone. Likewise, more than has been recognized, that which the ethicists say about their virtues also appears here. For they are unwilling that freedom, riches, honors, and health be regarded by their ethicist only to the extent that they are a help and instrument for exercising more conveniently and more easily the actions of virtue. But if ethics should transmit hypocrisy and pharisaism, of which further mention is made here, who, I ask, will be its auditor? *The difference between ethical and theological virtues is excellently set forth secondly according to Romans 1 and 2.* Nothing ethical is considered here, unless perhaps they wish the ethicist to communicate the catalogue of vices at the end of the first chapter. But by means of what front? The purpose (*scopus*) of the apostle elsewhere in these two chapters is to make it clear that all men are transgressors of the divine law and thus deserters of theological virtues.

117. These six arts perfect the whole man: logic directing his intellect; theology his will; and the remaining arts—grammar, rhetoric, mathematics, and physics—his locomotion according to rule in their eupraxiae.

118. With these six arts, the circle (κύκλος) or encyclopedia of education (παιδείας) and the arts is most perfectly completed and finished, receiving neither more nor less arts. Just as we have made this clear not only by the removal of those arts that others try in vain to include but also by a sufficient enumeration and attribution of the objects and laws of the true arts (by which they rightly come together), so we shall make this clear in that which follows.

119. Although we have introduced no explicit mention of those four preliminary disciplines (*praecognita*) that some force into encyclopedia beyond eleven sciences, five prudences, and seven arts, it is nevertheless evident from those things that have been said that archelogy and hexiology are included in technology

and are thus excluded with technology from the circle. But didactic, with respect to the whole circle and also with respect to this very technology or technometry, is as it were an external adjunct, and thus is so much further removed from the circle.

120. Among these six arts, theology, logic, and grammar contend for primacy. Theology precedes all the others in dignity; logic precedes in general necessity; nevertheless, in conformity with our manner of advancing, grammar initially takes the first parts [translator's note: the first parts or character roles on the stage] away from theology and logic, although in the ultimate end it is otherwise in dignity, as we have shown before.

121. No one man can use all these arts in every way; hence, there are certain uses of them and therefore faculties of using them acquired by artificers in this or that kind of life, about this or that object, useful in human life for this or that end. These uses and faculties of using are improperly and by metonomy accustomed to being called "arts," while they are absolutely and eminently called "faculties."

122. These faculties are distinguished into "more dignified" or "less dignified" from the greater or lesser dignity of their artificers and also of their object and end. Again, the "more dignified" are distinguished into "higher" and "lower," namely, insofar as the former in some way surpasses the latter.

123. The higher faculties are as follows: the theological, for gathering and building up the church of Christ; the juridical, for proclaiming law and administering justice; and the medical, fitted by nature for protecting and restoring men's health.

124. Here belong the jurisprudence enclosed in the *Corpus Juris* and any other writings of the civil laws. For, besides the customs and the ἄψυχα, nonrational pleasures of men (i.e., pleasures destitute of the reasons that are the force and soul of the laws), these survey nothing other than the faculty of certain distinguished jurists, whose faculty has been exercised in drawing forth from universal principles various conclusions of law and

equity, that is, in constituting special laws and judging various cases. These writings do not transmit the universal principles themselves, although they frequently, as occasion demands, take some of these principles from theology, for which, it has been shown, these universal principles are homogeneous. This is why the *Corpus Juris* and the writings of the civil laws do not constitute some new and distinct art or science (properly so called).

125. "From this we understand how undeservedly and unworthily everywhere today jurisconsults (*jurisconsulti*) are called (I should not say it!) 'prudent,' namely, those who, content with the *Corpus Juris* alone, are so little versed in the principles of our law that they do not seem to have tasted them with their upper lips or to have touched them with their fingers. For if knowing the laws is to grasp not their words but rather their force and power, as Celsus said in *On the Laws,* Book 17, 'Knowing the Laws,' who can say that he grasps the force and power of law when he is ignorant of its reason? Or what reason of law can there be which does not depend on the principles of law?" These words of the most celebrated jurisconsult Antoine Favre are deservedly to be applied not only here but also, with the proper changes, to the following faculties.

126. Here belong medicine or any kinds of medical writings that survey the faculty of distinguished physicians, whose faculty has been exercised in drawing forth particular medical conclusions from universal principles, that is, in making practical experiments and in prescribing various drugs. But medical writings themselves do not transmit the universal principles of healing; rather, they repeat for the given occasion the universal principles from physics (considered in its complete being, not in its defective existence). Therefore, medicine and medical writings constitute no new and distinct art.

127. The philosophical is called a lower faculty since it belongs τῶν τῆς σοφίας φίλων, to those loving wisdom, that is, to those who have not yet arrived but desire to arrive at wisdom itself,

which properly belongs to the higher faculties. Therefore, they pave the way for themselves, as it were, by this lower, acquired faculty.

128. There are, as it were, seven parts or partial faculties of this philosophical faculty: oratory, under which any kind of poetry falls; cosmography, in which is included astronomy and geography or the use of both globes; optics; music; architecture; economics; and politics.

129. Therefore, here belong the following systems: oratorical, poetical, cosmographical, astronomical, geographical, optical, musical, architectural, economical, and political. These systems survey the faculty of distinguished philosophers, whose faculty has been exercised in drawing forth particular philosophical conclusions (i.e., oratorical, poetical, cosmographical, etc.) by accommodation of the universal precepts of the arts. These systems do not transmit (or at least they ought not to transmit) new universal precepts that are not transmitted in the arts; but they frequently, by reason of the occasion, repeat them from the arts. Therefore, these systems constitute no new and distinct arts or sciences (properly so called).

130. Nonetheless, the reading and knowing of these systems contributes more than a little toward acquiring more easily and more rightly not only philosophy but also the higher faculties. Especially with respect to jurisprudence, there is great (although not principal) usefulness and necessity of geographical, architectural, household-economical, and political knowledge. We have not wanted to deny this in what has preceded.

131. The less dignified faculties are various: certainly, beyond those four just mentioned, all the remaining faculties honestly acquired and exercised by men. Experience testifies that none of these less dignified faculties ordinarily lifts its artificer to the summit of dignity as much as those four just mentioned.

132. Now these less dignified faculties (because of what we have said with respect to their being less dignified and in other respects) are called "sordid," "lucrative," "ignoble," "mechanical,"

"manual," and, eminently "productive," insofar as many of them are commonly acquired by their artificers for the sake of sordid gain, as it were, in a certain ignoble and servile manner. This is why it can be that among the ancients these less dignified faculties could have been considered proper to slaves and foreigners, as Zabarella and others note. They are also given the above names because they are exercised in doing things artificially with machines rather than by exercising natural talent. Nevertheless, there is not one of these that ought in itself to be unworthy of a naturally talented and free man, much less to seem base to anyone or render the body, spirit, or mind of anyone useless for the uses and actions of virtue.

133. For these less dignified faculties are effects of the arts (namely, of mathematics, almost all of them of physics, and a few of grammar), so that nothing ought to be imputed to them as such that should not be attributed by the same reason to the arts themselves, which are their causes. But he who predicates such things about the arts is in this predication certainly the most absurd of men.

134. It is indeed contradictory that something should be most necessary to promote the works of society (as much public as private) and yet render the body, spirit, and mind useless for the actions of virtue. Since such a thing as the latter is sin or the kindling of sin, it can therefore by no means be truly useful or necessary. Therefore, even the less equitable judges of these faculties should remove from them either the stain of disgrace or their necessity and usefulness. But since they have neither dared nor been able to remove the latter, they should therefore remove the former.

135. But these less dignified faculties are the effects of physics and grammar, not only insofar as they initiate them as their idea and model (*exemplar*)—considering the works of mathematics so that they may go astray less by imitating number, measure, and weight, that is, the just proportion of the parts in which there is the being of form—but also insofar as they borrow from one

or the other of them the matter of their works and the principal object of their exercise. Therefore, these less dignified faculties are most fittingly to be distinguished according to physics and grammar.

136. Therefore, some faculties or mechanical arts are grammatical, concerned with grammatical things; others are physical, concerned with physical things.

137. Those concerned with grammatical things have to do with the writing of letters, *either* elegantly in customary characters by pen or type, *or* quickly and briefly or covertly and secretly in uncustomary characters.

138. Calligraphy has to do with writing letters elegantly in customary characters with a pen. To calligraphy at the same time are to be referred the faculties of scribes of various kinds, clerks, secretaries, and similar persons who are, as it were, some particular progeny of calligraphy.

139. Typography has to do with writing letters in customary characters by type. From typography arises *libraria,* bookmanship, which either puts together those things that have been transcribed by type (this belongs to bookbinders), or preserves those things that have been stored away within the bookbinders' covers (this belongs to librarians).

140. Brachygraphy has to do with writing letters quickly and briefly in uncustomary characters. Brachygraphy devises new and easy-to-write characters, both separately in place of single letters and also jointly in place of several letters that compactly end or begin words. Brachygraphy then uses those characters that have been devised.

141. The so-called "art" of ciphers has to do with writing letters secretly and covertly in uncustomary characters. By means of this so-called "art" of ciphers, two or more persons by compact secretly communicate among themselves in writings things that they want read by no other. Yet this can also be done in customary characters by one who has had the way explained to him

by Baron Verulam in *On the Dignity and Augmentations of the Sciences* (book 6, chapter 1).

142. Paper-making (*chartopoeia*) and parchment-making (*pergamenopoeia*) are subordinate to and serve all these grammatical faculties, preparing for them paper and parchments on which letters are written today.

143. The faculties concerned with physical matters have to do either with the elements (fire, air, water, and earth) or with those things composed of the elements (*elementata*). And again, both of these have to do either with the things themselves or with their qualities.

144. The faculties concerned with fire have to do with skillfully starting it, settling it, preserving it, spreading it, conveniently communicating it to others, etc. Here belong all those military arts of cannon, gunpowder, and cannon balls insofar as they are in some way or another occupied with fire. Here likewise belong the arts of artificial lights, and also those of heated bathing rooms, ovens, and similar things that serve by preserving and conveniently communicating fire.

145. The faculties concerned with air have to do with stirring it up, calming it, infecting it, purifying it, and blowing it by means of bellows.

146. The faculties concerned with water have to do with containing it within its boundaries by constructed dams, dispersing it from place to place, elevating it, swimming in it, inhabiting it so to speak for a time (which belongs to divers), and navigating it. From navigating comes the nautical art that, insofar as it gathers winds in sails, is also occupied with air.

147. The faculties concerned with earth have to do with plowing it, harrowing it, digging it up, or preparing it in other ways. A certain part of agriculture and of gardening is in these faculties, namely, the faculty of the plowman, of the harrower, of the digger, of the planter, etc.

148. The faculties concerned with the qualities of the elements

have to do either with primary qualities (i.e., the faculty of heating, of cooling, of drying, of moistening) or with secondary qualities (i.e., the faculty of solidifying, of liquifying, of condensing, of rarefying.)

149. The faculties concerned with the qualities of things composed of the elements have to do with *color,* the faculty of painting and of dyeing; *sound,* the faculty of instrumental music, which is varied because of the variety of instruments, namely, the faculty of the harpist, of the lutist, of the organist, of the lyrist, of the trumpeter, of the clarion blower, of the bugler, of the cithara player, of the pandura player, of the nablium player, of the flute player, of the tympanist, of the cornet player, of the bagpiper, etc.; *taste,* the faculty of cooking, especially of the preparation of delicacies; *smell,* the faculty of perfuming and of the florist, insofar as he puts plants together for fragrance.

150. The faculties concerned with the things themselves composed of the elements have to do either with inanimate things (stones, metals, and minerals of a median nature) or with living things.

151. The faculties concerned with stones have to do either with *precious* stones (the faculty of the jeweler, the stonecutter, and the engraver of precious stones) or with *more common* stones. These latter faculties have to do with *natural* stones, namely, quarrying them, liquifying them, and pouring them out like bronze, shaping them, and engraving them (these last two faculties are of the cutter and of the engraver); and with *baked* stones (the faculty of the brickmaker and afterwards of the road maker and of the wall builder).

152. The faculties concerned with metals are as much about metals *in general,* namely, mining them, washing them, examining them, distinguishing them, smelting them, polishing them (these faculties belong to metallurgists working in the mines) as about metals *in specific,* namely, gold, silver, bronze, iron, copper, tin, and lead.

153. Concerned with gold and silver are goldbeating; gold-

smithing (in which there is gilding with gold, engraving, and ring-making); and minting coins.

154. Concerned with bronze are the casting of bronze utensils, of bells, of military engines, etc.

155. Concerned with iron is any kind of ironsmithing, namely, the faculty of the lock maker, the sword maker, the maker of lime burners, the maker of armor, the maker of weapons, the knife maker, the sickle maker, etc.

156. Coppersmithing is concerned with copper; tinsmithing with tin; plumbing with lead.

157. The faculties concerned with minerals of a median nature have to do with drying out and preparing salt (the salt trade); clay (the potters' trade); and glass (the glass trade).

158. The faculties concerned with living things have to do either with plants or animals; the latter are concerned either with rational animals (namely, men) or with brute animals.

159. The faculties concerned with plants have to do with *herbage,* first of the gardener and the botanist, then of the dealer in spices, and also, by some reason, of the cook and the florist; with *fruits,* namely, sowing them and cultivating them into ears of grain (agriculture), reaping, gathering, threshing, and process-ing (milling, grinding, and brewing); with *grapevines,* namely, the faculty of the dresser, the pruner, the trimmer, the grape gatherer, and the wine presser; with *trees,* namely, the faculty of the pruner, the grafter, the fruit seller with respect to the fruit, and woodworking of every kind (the faculty of the box maker, the ship builder, the lathe turner, the basket maker, the carpen-ter, the maker of statues, the maker of bows, and the charcoal burner with respect to wood). Hemp and flax are also classified with plants; here, therefore, certainly belong any occupations concerned with hemp or flax (rope-making, thread-making, and the like).

160. The faculties concerned with brute animals have to do with aerial animals (birds); or aquatic animals (fish); or ter-restrial animals (domestic or wild).

161. The faculties concerned with birds have to do with catching them, namely, the faculty of catching birds of various kinds (e.g., the duck keeper, the dove keeper); keeping them; and training them.

162. Concerned with fish are fishing with casting nets, large fishing nets, javelins, wicker baskets, plaited hampers, basins, fishhooks, and other instruments (all called by the one name, "fishing"); and keeping them in fish ponds or aquaria.

163. The faculties concerned with domestic animals have to do with pasturing them (the faculty of the oxherd, the swineherd, the shepherd, and the goatherd); or with fattening them for slaughter (the faculty of the stockman); with slaughtering them (the faculty of the butcher); or with putting them to other uses as beasts of burden. Here belongs the faculty of the stable groom, the one who drives and takes care of horses, the one who drives and takes care of mules, the wagon driver, and those who, as it were, serve them by either furnishing the beasts of burden with necessary things (the faculty of the horse-cloth maker, of the whip maker, and of the saddle maker, who themselves have handicraftsmen who are subservient to themselves); or curing their ills (the faculty of the veterinarian, etc.).

164. The faculty of the hunter has to do with capturing wild animals with hounds, snares, nooses, or enclosures; and with keeping them in preserves.

165. The faculties concerned with man have to do with his body. They have to do with *clothing*—with respect to the head, the faculty of hat making; with respect to the hands, glove making; with respect to the feet, cobbling (making shoes as much as making sandals), for which the tanner also furnishes leather; with respect to the rest of the body, the faculty of clothiers (who in some places also clothe the head and the hands of men), the tailor and all those who prepare materials for him (such as the silk dealers, ornament dealers, any kind of wool workers, and spinners, namely, plaiters or weavers, cloth fullers, and others of this kind)—or with *exercising* for agility, wrestling,

boxing, the faculty of running, ball games, etc.; or with *healing,* surgery, the faculty of the stone cutter, the dealer in ointment, all of which, along with pharmacy (which especially belongs here), are subordinate to medicine; or with *cleaning,* bathing, barbering.

166. Even if these are not all, these are at least many of the faculties that men acquire for themselves in their own manner from the arts (some from known and applied precepts of the arts, some from written transmission, some from transmission through the hands of artificers).

167. But, lest anyone be able to say vainly that he has some ability in these things and often be able to do much harm, and since he ought to be productive, it has been prudently constituted that certain men distinguished in the principal faculties test, approve and by their testimony honor the approved candidates of those faculties.

168. This is why there are those academic degrees: He who has been found by a previous examination and trial to be excelling in the philosophical faculty is solemnly pronounced a *Master of Liberal Arts* or a *Doctor of Philosophy;* in the medical faculty, a *Doctor of Medicine;* in the juridical faculty, a *Doctor of Jurisprudence;* in the theological faculty, a *Doctor of Theology,* by the presiding doctors of the same faculty in some university. The one who is found so excelling is given by the highest magistrate of the same university the full power of exercising that faculty everywhere as the occasion arises.

169. This is why a trial work (*tyrocinium, ein Meisterstück*) must be made by the individual workers of Germany who want to be occupied freely in some privileged work and do not want to be annoyed or hindered by colleagues of their work.

COMMENTARY

Commentary

Thesis 1. Ames sets forth the nature of art in terms of its definition. Cf. his definition of art in general in the Prologue of the *Demonstratio Logicae Verae*, thesis 4, p. 121: "Art is the regular disposition or instruction of a thing, in existence and operation, agreeably to its end." Ames elsewhere says that this definition of art comprehends the four common prerequisites for constituting any art: "genus, difference, matter of the genus, and form of the genus" (*Alia Technometriae Delineatio,* thesis 6, pp. 45–46). This definition of art in general is an abstraction from the six individual arts that constitute encyclopedia, and the form of this definition applies commonly to each of the six arts.

Thesis 2. In theses 2–12 Ames clarifies and limits what he means by art as "idea," which is the "genus" or "the primary essence" common to all the arts. The Greek phrase τῶν μέσων, translated "ambiguous," literally means "of indeterminate things"; for a similar usage of these words with regard to the ambiguity of the word "art," see Honoratus Maurus Servius's commentary on Virgil's *Aeneid*, in *Pub. Vergilii Maronis Opera . . . Omnia* (Basel, 1695), cols. 523–24.

Thesis 3. Ames follows his master Ramus in accepting Aristotle's moderate realism rather than Plato's objective idealism or realism with regard to man's knowledge of universal ideas; cf. Ramus, *Scholae metaphysicae,* bk. 1, chap. 5, in *Scholae in lib-*

erales artes (Basel, 1559), col. 847; also Ames, "Theses Physiologicae," chap. 55, theses 9–10, in the student notebook of John
Clark, p. 37. This Aristotelian "empiricism" should be modified
in the light of the strongly Platonic cast of Ames's discussion of
the idea of art in God (see theses 15 and 43, below) and of his
discussion of "ideas" with respect to God and man (*Marrow of
Theology,* bk. 1, chap. 7, theses 14–23, pp. 95–96). Ames really
attempts to synthesize the Aristotelian and Platonic positions on
the existence and knowledge of universals or general ideas; see,
for example, Ames's Prologomena to *Demonstratio Logicae
Verae,* thesis 4, p. 121. Furthermore, interpreting the primary
essence of "idea" in terms of its final cause or "end," Ames
attempts to synthesize the medieval "intellectualist" and "voluntarist" schools. This same teleological understanding of "idea" is
reiterated below in theses 12 and 39. The reference to Plautus
(c. 251–184 B.C.) is taken from a passing comment by the Roman
poet Horace (c. 65–8 B.C.): "Plautus hurries along like his model
[*exemplar*], Epicharmus of Sicily . . ." (*Epistle to Augustus,* in
Satires, Epistles, and Ars Poetica, trans. H. R. Fairclough, Loeb
Classical Library [New York: G. P. Putnam's Sons, 1926], pp.
400–01). Epicharmus was a Greek comic poet of Megara in Sicily
who lived in the sixth and fifth centuries B.C.

Thesis 4. There is no ultimate possibility in Ames's thought
for an agent to act "by chance." God not only creates according
to but continues to govern in his providence by means of the
principles of art (see theses 43–45, below). Natural things (that
is, nonrational agents) are determined by the inner necessity of
their natures to act in conformity with the principles, law, or will
of God (*Marrow of Theology,* bk. 1, chap. 9, theses 22–25, pp.
109–10; see also *Conscience,* bk. 5, chap. 1, theses 13–15, p. 102).
Rational agents (angels and men) participate in the law or will
of God by acting from reason and counsel (*Marrow of Theology,*
bk. 1, chap. 7, theses 11 and 13, p. 95).

Thesis 5. Ames lists the other "parts" that make up the "whole"
of art. Although all of the terms mentioned play vital roles in
Ames's thought, he rejects them as definitions of art because they
are causes, effects, or adjuncts, but not the general essence of art,
which is "idea."

Thesis 6. Ames is playing on the derivation of the word "habit" [*habitus*] from *habeo*, which means "to have" or "to possess"; cf. the similar case in Greek where ἕξις, "habit," is derived from ἔχω, "I am able" or "I have." Ames is rejecting Aristotle and his followers, who define art as "a habit capable of making according to true reason" (*Nichomachean Ethics* 6.3.6, Loeb ed., p. 334; however, cf. Ames's qualified approval of this definition of art in thesis 33, below. See also Ames, *Conscience*, bk. 1, chap. 1, thesis 5, p. 3; and Alexander Richardson, "Rhetorical Notes," in *The Logicians School-Master*, p. 65.

Thesis 7. The terms dealt with in theses 7 and 8—"art," "discipline," "science," "understanding," "book," and "virtue," especially prudence and wisdom—had long been associated with each other; e.g., see Aristotle *Nichomachean Ethics* 6.3.1, pp. 330–33, Alexander Richardson shows how all of these terms are related to one another in Ramist thought in *The Logicians School-Master*, p. 23; cf. Ames, Prologomena to *Demonstratio Logicae Verae*, thesis 2, p. 121.

Thesis 8. Ames argues against defining art as a virtue because virtue per se is not taught in common by all the individual arts but only by theology (see theses 113–16, below). And "science" cannot define the primary essence of art because it is only one of several prerequisites for art (see theses 79 and 84). Furthermore, for Ames, "science" is not a virtue but only a judgment of the intellect that leads or helps the will toward virtuous action. In rejecting the derivation of the Latin *ars*, "art," from the Greek ἀρετή, Ames is going against the commentator Servius in the *Aeneid* (see *Pub. Vergilii Maronis Opera . . . Omnia*, col. 971); against Augustine in *De Civitate Dei*, 4.21; and against Aurelius Cassiodorus in Praefatio, *De Artibus ac Disciplinis Liberalium Artium* (J. P. Migne, *Patrologiae Latinae*, Vol. 70, col. 1151). Ames prefers the derivation of *ars* from *arx*, "tower" or *artus*, "sinew" (see thesis 41, below; also *Alia Technometriae Delineatio*, thesis 15, p. 47).

Thesis 9. Having argued that the common genus of art is "idea," Ames turns to the second prerequisite of art, namely, "eupraxia," the common difference that differentiates the individual arts. "Eupraxia" is a transliteration of the Greek εὐπραξία, which is made up of the adverb εὖ, "well," and πρᾶξις, "doing," "action," or "exercise." Aristotle uses the word "eupraxia" in discussing his definition of happiness; see *Nichomachean Ethics* 1.8.4, pp. 36–39. Ramus approves of Aristotle's usage of the word in *Prooemium Reformandae Parisiensis Academiae,* in *Collectaneae,* pp. 486–87. Ames himself translates "eupraxia" simply as *bona actio,* "good action," in *Alia Technometriae Delineatio,* thesis 22, p. 49. In conformity with the translations of the Ramist definitions of the individual arts, it is probably best translated as "doing or making well," "practicing well." Ames gives his formal definition below in thesis 13. Here he is still concerned with defining and delimiting "idea" by introducing eupraxia as the object and end of art.

Thesis 10. Ames rejects the position of those who hold that the object of art is the mind and will of an individual man, for art is not primarily in human subjects but in the mind of God and in created things. Science, habit, and virtue, however, are primarily in the heads and hearts of men. Ames must also reject the position that guidance or direction of the mind and the will is the object and end of art because guidance and direction have already been made part of the general essence of "art" as "idea."

Thesis 11. In spite of the primacy of art's objectivity in the mind of God and in created things, Ames does not want to belittle or deny the subjective appropriation of art. And insofar as art is subjectively appropriated by men, their minds and wills are directed by it.

Thesis 12. This thesis summarizes theses 2–10 and ends Ames's discussion of art as "idea." He now turns to the nature of eupraxia in terms of its definition and division or distribution.

Thesis 13. Ames's formal definition of eupraxia is similar to that of Alexander Richardson: "Practice is the motion of an art in acting" (*The Logicians School-Master,* p. 27). The adjective "regular" modifying "motion" in Ames's definition means "motion according to rule or principle." Most Ramists treat motion primarily as a part of logic and only derivatively or in a "borrowed" sense as a part of physics; e.g., see William Temple, *De Physicis nonnullis Pro P. Ramo, contra Lieblerum,* in *Pro Mildapetti de unica methodo defensione contra Diplodophilum*

(London, 1581), p. 1. Motion in Ramist logic was from composites to simples (analysis) or vice-versa (genesis). Ames and Richardson went beyond earlier Ramists in holding that motion is not even to be transmitted first in logic but rather in a prefatorial introduction to the art of logic (Richardson) or in technometry (Ames).

Thesis 14. Ames traces the imperfection of eupraxia in the art of men not to the objectivity of art in things but to its subjective appropriation and use by men. The imperfection of the arts in men and the weakness of the human powers required for eupraxia are explained by Ames and Richardson in terms of man's sin, which occurred first and decisively in the fall of the first man, Adam; see thesis 61, below, and *The Logicians School-Master,* pp. 37, 39–40.

Thesis 15. In this thesis Ames firmly grounds the objectivity of art in things and in the mind of God. This is Ames's solution to the age-old problem of the one and the many; see also *Marrow of Theology* bk. 1, chap. 4, thesis 53, p. 87; bk. 1, chap. 7, theses 19 and 23, p. 96; and Richardson, *The Logicians School-Master,* p. 5. In spite of his rejection of metaphysics as an independent discipline, Ames agrees with Richardson in holding that being (*ens*) is the subject of all art. Both Ames and Richardson dichotomize being into "First Being" (that is, God) and "being derived from First Being" (that is, the creatures); see Prologomena to *Demonstratio Logicae Verae,* thesis 4, p. 121; *The Logicians School-Master,* pp. 4 ff. But since First Being is beyond man's reason, being derived from First Being is the proper and adequate subject of human reason and of all of man's arts. And since the concrete manifestations of being derived from First Being are various and manifold, derivative or created being is so perceived by man in the several individual arts. In spite of Ames's use of this metaphorical language of "being derived or emanating from First Being" for conceiving of God as the Creator of the world, he always prefers and returns to the metaphor of the artist fashioning his artifact as the most preeminent, satisfactory, and biblical; see *The Substance of the Christian Religion* (London, 1659), pp. 66–67.

Thesis 16. Ames proceeds to the distribution or division of

eupraxia in general. "Eupraxia is divided into its parts and species, and it has joined to itself the euprattomenon (εὐπραττόμενον) or the work made by its motion" (*Alia Technometriae Delineatio,* thesis 8, p. 46; cf. thesis 28, p. 51). Theses 16–21 of *Technometry* deal with the "parts" of eupraxia; theses 22–31 deal with its species; and theses 31–36 deal with its adjunct or "euprattomenon." The two parts of eupraxia are "genesis" and "analysis." Aristotle knew about these methods, which were current among geometers of his time, and Plato may have been familiar with them too. There is also a direct relation between Ramus's understanding of genesis and analysis and that of the medical tradition, as represented by the three orderly teaching procedures of Galen, namely, analysis, synthesis, and the dismemberment of definitions; see Ramus, *Animadversionum Aristotelicarum, Libri XX* (Paris, 1549), p. 349. When Ramus takes over the terms "genesis" and "analysis," he is thinking and acting primarily as a humanist pedagogue. Ramus applies these terms to the composition and disposition of the content matter of an art, and thereby to his method of teaching art in the classroom; see Ramus, *Pro Philosophica Parisiensis Academiae disciplina Oratio,* in *Collectaneae,* pp. 326–27. Since genesis and analysis are common to all arts and are a part of the exercise of eupraxia in every art, Ames deals with them in the context of his discussion of art in general. The Latin words *ad vivum,* translated in thesis 16 adverbially as "vitally," literally mean "to the quick"; cf. Richardson's statement that genesis and analysis are "the life of Art" in *The Logicians School-Master,* p. 30. Ames explains in thesis 19 what he means by genesis and analysis expressing vitally the reciprocation of eupraxia's motion.

Thesis 17. This is the definition of genesis; cf. Richardson's definition in *The Logicians School-Master,* p. 28.

Thesis 18. This is the definition of analysis; cf. Richardson's definition in *The Logicians School-Master,* p. 29.

Thesis 19. Ames sets forth the Ramist position that genesis is analysis in reverse. Genesis reassembles the simples or individuals that analysis breaks down or resolves. Ames agrees with Ramus in identifying the reciprocal motion of genesis and analysis with the logical procedures of induction and deduction. This understanding of analysis in terms of logical induction is not only compatible with but helped to clear the path for the empirical, observational, and experimental method of scientific inquiry. See Ames's further elaboration of analysis and his approval of the experimental method of Francis Bacon in theses 69 and 70, below.

Thesis 20. The Ramist understanding of "imitation" is governed by the procedure of teaching and learning the arts in the classroom. Ramus teaches that genesis or composition begins with the imitation of analysis in reverse. After one has learned by close imitation, he may then move on to expressions of greater freedom. See Ramus, *Dialectici comm. tres* (1546), p. 110, quoted and translated by Ong, *Ramus,* p. 264; see also Richardson, *The Logicians School-Master,* p. 30.

Thesis 21. This thesis is an intimate part of the preceding thesis on "imitation." Ames is asserting that imitation, like genesis and analysis, is to be taught in this "place" concerning art in general because it is common to all of the arts. Therefore, although used by all the individual arts, imitation cannot be taught as belonging uniquely or especially to any one individual art. The second part of thesis 21 explains why genesis and analysis in general can only be taught in the "place" where art in general is being taught, namely, because every individual art pursues the teaching of the special analysis and genesis that is appropriate to it and therefore does not teach about genesis and analysis in general. This assertion that individual arts are ordered with their beginning in special analysis and genesis underscores the Ramist tenet that the principles of art are "found" or derived inductively by analysis and then "imitated" by genesis or composition.

Thesis 22. Ames now turns to distributing the species of eupraxia, namely, general eupraxia and special eupraxia. This movement from the generic to the specific is one of the most characteristic features of Ramist thought and teaching. One of the most basic Ramist tenets is that even though knowledge must begin with individuals, genera are really "more known" or are "clearer to reason" than individuals. This Ramist tenet is derived from Aristotle, who distinguishes between that which is prior and more knowable by nature (that is, the most universal concept) and that which is prior and more knowable in relation to us (that is, that which is nearer to our perception); see *Posterior Analytics* 1.2, trans. Hugh Tredenick, Loeb Classical Library (Cambridge, Mass.: Harvard University Press, 1960), pp. 30–33. This Ramist position about genera being "more knowable" comes out clearly in all discussions of "method"; cf. Ames, *Demonstratio Logicae Verae,* theses 125–26, p. 155. In thesis 22 of *Technometry,* Ames is careful to point out that "general" and "special" are species of the one genus, eupraxia. The terms "general" and "special" refer to the use of the six species of eupraxia, three of which are more or less general and three of which are less or more special. In speaking of the "use" of eupraxia in this thesis, Ames means primarily the use of one or more of the more general eupraxia by other, more specific eupraxiae. What Ames means by the general eupraxiae "becoming concrete" in the special is clarified in theses 23–31, where he sets forth the six species of eupraxia that differentiate the six individual arts.

Thesis 23. Ames argues that the more general eupraxia of "discoursing well" distinguishes logic not only from the other two general arts of communication (grammar and rhetoric) but also from the special arts (mathematics, physics, and theology). Ramus and all of his followers liked to claim Cicero as the fount of the definition of logic or dialectic as "the art of discoursing well." The Latin verb *dissero* not only implies "discoursing" but also "arguing" and "reasoning," as is also the case with the deponent Greek verb διαλέγομαι; see Cicero *De Fato* 1.1, trans. H. Rackham, Loeb Classical Library (Cambridge, Mass.: Harvard University Press, 1942), pp. 192–93. A second passage from Cicero shows not only the ambiguity in the word *dissero* but also the source of the Ramist dichotomization of dialectic into invention and disposition of judgment in Cicero himself; see *Topica* 2.6, trans. H. M. Hubbell, Loeb Classical Library (Cambridge, Mass.: Harvard University Press, 1959), pp. 386–87. By making no distinction between "dialectic" and "logic" (see Ramus, *Animadversionum Aristotelicarum Libri XX,* p. 19), Ramus and his followers were opposing Aristotle and the Peripatetics who divide logic into a apodictic, dialectic, and sophistic. They were also opposing the Stoics, who make logic the genus and then divide it into dialectic and rhetoric; see George Downame, In *Petri Rami . . . Dialecticam Commentarii,* pp. 68–69. By identifying logic and dialectic, Ramus and his followers conceive of dialectic in terms of Aristotle's *Topics;* for Aristotle himself, dialectic dealt with probable argumentation and for Cicero it led to establishing belief [*fides*] in matters about which there is some doubt. This explains much of the "argumentative" (as opposed to "demonstrative") language used in Ramist logic. The division of logic into invention and disposition or judgment also shows the intimate association of Ramist logic with the Ciceronian rhetorical tradition.

Thesis 24. In theses 24–26 Ames sets forth the priority of logic in terms of absolute or general necessity, which is contrasted with the hypothetical necessity of the two less general eupraxiae in thesis 25. The rationalism of the Ramist position is clearly explicated in these theses. Logic is "the art of arts" and "the key to all the other arts." See Richardson, *The Logicians School-Master,* pp. 10–11; also Ramus, *Pro Philosophica Parisiensis academiae disciplina Oratio,* in *Collectaneae,* p. 347.

Thesis 25. Ames introduces the other two (less) general eupraxiae that, along with dialectic, make up the complete Ramist theory of communication, namely, "speaking" (grammar) and "communicating" (rhetoric); see Ramus, *Scholarum Rhetoricarum Liber III,* in *Scholae in Liberales Artes,* col. 269. For the Ramists, grammar is concerned with speaking purely or correctly, while rhetoric is concerned with speaking sweetly or ornately. There is difficulty involved in translating into English the two Latin terms for expressing the eupraxiae that distinguish grammar and rhetoric. Both *loquor* and *dico* come over into English as "speak" or "say." Richardson explains what is involved in the two verbs *loquor* and *dico* in such a way that rhetoric is shown to be intimately connected with the orator pleading his case in court before a judge, as is the case in the rhetoric of Aristotle and Cicero (*Grammatical Notes,* pp. 13–14; also *Rhetorical Notes,* p. 30). Although the word "communicate" applies to dialectic and grammar as well as to rhetoric (as is also the case with "speak"), the word does include both writing and utterance that have become ornate through the use of tropes and figures. Rhetoric as the *ars bene dicendi* has thus been translated as "the art of communicating well." What Ames means by "the image" of the former general eupraxia is clarified by his definition of an "image" in the context of his discussion of man being made in "the image of God" (*Marrow of Theology,* bk. 1, chap. 8, thesis 66, p. 105). Both Ramus and Ames argue that grammar and rhetoric cannot contend with dialectic in generality of use, and further that grammar is prior to rhetoric; see Ramus, *Scholarum Rhetoricarum Liber III,* in *Scholae in Liberales Artes,* col. 282.

Thesis 26. The fact that grammar and rhetoric are subordinated to the status of handmaidens of logic again reveals the controlling influence of logic as the Ramist key to all the other arts; see thesis 102, below, where Ames calls grammar and rhetoric "associates" and "handmaidens." The statement that logic has "better being" in man is not only a judgment about the ontological priority and status of the dialectical art but, more accurately, a descriptive concrete judgment that man is by nature or by art a better logician than he is a grammarian or rhetorician. The reasons for the "worse being" of grammar and rhetoric are given below in theses 101 and 102.

Thesis 27. In theses 27–31 Ames takes up the three special eupraxiae that distinguish the arts of mathematics, physics, and theology. These special eupraxiae necessarily presuppose and use the general eupraxiae, but not vice-versa. The transition between general and special eupraxiae is also the transition between the traditional *trivium* of the liberal arts faculty—logic, grammar, and rhetoric—and the revised Ramist version of the *quadrivium*—traditionally arithmetic, geometry, music, and astronomy.

Thesis 28. This thesis sets forth the three special eupraxiae that distinguish the arts of mathematics, physics, and theology. Ames reflects little or no real interest in mathematics, and he does not even mention the Ramist division of mathematics into two parts, arithmetic and geometry. Ames's definition of the art of mathematics reflects the Ramist definition of geometry as *ars bene metiendi,* "the art of measuring well." For Ramus, mathematics is the general art of quantity, or "quantifying well." Although Ramus was a humanist with a strong bent toward dialectic and rhetoric, he was much enamoured with and spent several years of his later study in the pursuit of mathematics; see his *Scholarum Mathematicarum Liber IV* and the English translation of his *The Way to Geometry* (London, 1636). Moreover, Ramus's revision of the traditional *quadrivium* is of tremendous historical importance. Rejecting the traditional arrangement of the *quadrivium* into arithmetic, geometry, music, and astronomy, he preferred to consider arithmetic and geometry as parts of the one art of mathematics, while assigning music and astronomy to the one art of physics; see his *Scholarum Mathematicarum Liber IV*, pp. 113–14. After Ramus, astronomy, harmony, and optics are treated as a part of physics and not as a part of mathematics. That Ames is in accord with Ramus on this question is clearly seen in theses 107 and 108, below. The translation of *bene naturandi* as "doing the work of nature well" is based on a text from Alexander Richardson: *"Bene naturandi.*] i.e. to do the work of nature well" (*Notes of Physicks*, p. 87). The use of the active voice of the verb *naturo*, which usually occurs in the passive voice as *nascor*, "to be born" or "to be produced," shows that the active voice was in usage before Benedict Spinoza (1633–77) made his influential distinction between *Natura naturans* and *Natura naturata* (see Spinoza, "God, Man, and His Well-Being," in *Spinoza Selections*, ed. John Wild (New York: Charles Scribner's Sons, 1958), pp. 80–81). In fact, Ames himself makes the distinction between *Natura naturans* and *Natura naturata* in the first two theses of chapter 1, "On Nature," in his "Theses Physiologicae," p. 37. Ames and Spinoza are in agreement in seeing *Natura naturans* as the first cause of all things. They differ, however, insofar as for Ames *Natura naturans* (that is, God) transcends the created realm of *Natura naturata*, while Spinoza's immanent God (*Natura naturans*) exists only in and through its modes (*Natura naturata*) and includes them rather than simply transcends them. The fundamental idea behind the Ramist understanding of physics as the art of doing the work of nature well is that man can imitate nature by means of learning and applying the art of physics. For the Ramists, the art of physics deals with the whole realm of nature, and nature (*Natura naturata*) includes everything except God; see Richardson, *Notes of Physicks*, p. 88. Ramus wrote no formal treatise on the art of physics, for his *Scholarum Physicarum Libri* were primarily in criticism of Aristotle's *Physics* as being more about logic and metaphysics than about physics. Nevertheless, he does outline what he conceives to be included within the art in his commentary on Vergil's pastoral poem, *The Georgics;* see *P. Vergilii Maronis Georgica* (Paris, 1564), pp. 17–18. Ames's "Theses Physiologicae" briefly set forth the entire spectrum of the art of physics as Ramus conceived of it. The special eupraxia of "living well" distinguishes the art of theology. Yet, for reasons alluded to in thesis 110, below, Ames prefers to speak of theology as "teaching" (*doctrina*) rather than as "art" (*ars*). This understanding of theology as "living well" is implicit in the opening sentence of the *Marrow of Theology:* "Divinity is the doctrine of living to God. . . . εὖζω, to live well, is more excellent than εὐδαιμονεῖν, to live happily" (bk. 1, chap. 1, theses 1, 5–6, 8, pp. 78–79). Ramus was undoubtedly the source of Ames's understanding of theology: "Theology is the teaching of living well . . ." (*Commentarium de Religione Christiana,* bk. 1, chap. 1 [Frankfort, 1576], pp. 6–7).

Thesis 29. Ames argues, in good Ramist fashion, that the special eupraxiae do not "mix with" or become concrete in the general eupraxiae, while the general eupraxiae do become "mixed with" or concrete in the special eupraxiae.

Thesis 30. Ames clarifies his distinction between less and more special eupraxiae. Of the special eupraxiae, Ramists always insist that theology is "the most special of all the arts"; see Ramus, *Scholarum Metaphysicarum Liber I,* in *Scholae in Liberales Artes,* col. 834; Richardson, *The Logicians School-Master,* p. 69. This is a profound new interpretation of the comprehensiveness and importance of theology as the most dignified of the arts and sciences. None of the other arts presuppose or need theology, and yet theology presupposes and uses all of the other arts. Nevertheless, in a very real sense all of the other arts are "for the sake of" the art or teaching of theology.

Thesis 31. This thesis refers back to thesis 14. Even though the aptitude of a eupraxia may be very weak and imperfect in men, that eupraxia does not cease being the object and end of an art. Ames explains in thesis 71, below, why doing the work of nature has been the most imperfect of all the arts in men. In thesis 61 he explains why the eupraxia of living well is so weak and imperfect in men.

Thesis 32. Having now divided eupraxia into its parts (genesis and analysis) and into its species (general and special), Ames now turns his attention to the *euprattomenon,* the work made by the motion of eupraxia (theses 32–36). The word "euprattomenon" is a transliteration from the Greek εὐπραττόμενον, which literally means "that which has been made well or done well." The use of this word is simply another way of speaking about the art object made by an artist, that is, an artifact. The point is simply that there can be no artistic activity (that is, eupraxia) that does not produce or make an artifact (that is, a euprattomenon); cf. Richardson, *The Logicians School-Master,* pp. 25–26. This assertion that every eupraxia must necessarily have its euprattomenon lays the foundation for the rejection of the distinction between arts that are theoretical (not concerned with practice and thereby implicitly having no euprattomenon) and those that are practical (concerned with doing and making).

Thesis 33. Ames gives qualified approval to Aristotle's definition of art as "a habit capable of making according to true reason" (see *Nichomachean Ethics* 6.4, pp. 334–73). Ames is saying something different from Aristotle here, for Aristotle is applying the word "art" more narrowly to that which is variable (in contrast to the necessity and unchangeableness of scientific knowledge). Secondly, Aristotle is making a distinction between doing (πρᾶξις) and making (ποίησις). The essential point that Ames is after in quoting Aristotle is that all art deals with bringing something into existence, and that to pursue an art means to study how to bring into existence a thing that lies in the maker and not in the thing made. Richardson, in stressing that every thing has its *praxis* and *prattomenon* given to it by its Creator, gives a list of the prattomena of the different arts that partially parallels that given by Ames in thesis 33; see *The Logicians School-Master,* p. 27.

Thesis 34. Ames is still concerned in this thesis with Aristotle's distinction between "making" (ποίησις) and "action" or "doing" (πρᾶξις), even though he himself does not accept the distinction;

cf. *Alia Technometriae Delineatio,* thesis 41, p. 54; and Richardson, *The Logicians School-Master,* pp. 26–27. For an example of the position Ames and Richardson oppose, see Alsted's division of the disciplines into (1) theoretical or contemplative, (2) practical or active, and (3) poetic or effective (*Encyclopaedia,* vol. 1, bk. 1, chap. 7, p. 52). For this opposing school of Aristotle and his followers, "contemplation" ($\theta\epsilon\omega\rho\iota\alpha$) and "doing" ($\pi\rho\hat{\alpha}\xi\iota s$) take place according to the inner necessity of man's nature as a rational and political animal. They argue that "making" ($\pi o\iota\eta\sigma\iota s$) has to do with the changeable and variable, and must be external and "perceptible to the senses." Ames and Richardson not only reject this reduction of "making" to producing something that is "perceptible to the senses" but also, and even more importantly, this narrow and inadequate view of "art."

Thesis 35. Ames holds that there are two "properties" of euprattomenon, namely, "use" and "abstraction"; see *Alia Technometriae Delineatio,* thesis 42, p. 54. In this thesis Ames is dealing with the first "property" of euprattomenon, its use. In thesis 36 he deals with its second "property," abstraction. There is an almost identical passage in Richardson, where a similar example is used to illustrate the common and confused use of euprattomena, even though they are clear and distinct per se; see *The Logicians School-Master,* p. 31.

Thesis 36. The second "property" of euprattomenon is abstraction. By means of the speculative or abstractive power of the mind, the various prattomena that are common and confused in use are isolated or separated from one another. They are then seen to be clear and distinct as they really are among themselves, and every prattomenon can then be assigned to its own eupraxia, discipline, or art; cf. *Alia Technometriae Delineatio,* 43, pp. 54–55. There is a striking similarity between abstracting and separating speculation, which breaks down those prattomena that are common and confused in use, and analysis, which is one of the integral parts of eupraxia and which regularly regresses from composites to simples; see thesis 18, above.

Thesis 37. Ames has now, in his discussion of art in terms of its definition, considered the common genus of all the arts ("idea") and the common difference of all the arts ("eupraxia").

Eupraxia has been divided or distributed into its parts (genesis and analysis) and species (general and special). Finally, euprattomenon (the work made by the motion of eupraxia) has been presented as the inevitable adjunct of eupraxia and in terms of its two properties, use and abstraction. Having discussed "Art is the idea of eupraxia" in theses 2–36, in theses 37–87 Ames discusses the second half of the definition, that art is "methodically delineated by universal rules." Ames uses the word "delineate" (*delineo*) in thesis 37 to mean "represent clearly and accurately" the idea of eupraxia by means of many delineations or lines. Ames asserts that these delineations (or "rules," as he prefers to call them in thesis 39, below) are the "matter" of art; see *Alia Technometriae Delineatio,* thesis 9, p. 46; also George Downame, *In Petri Rami . . . Dialecticam Commentarii,* p. 27. Ames repeats in thesis 37 the assertion he made in thesis 15, before dividing eupraxia into its parts and species: that eupraxia exists in God or in the exercise of God as one unique and most simple art. Ames repeats this assertion because he is preparing to speak of not one delineation but many delineations that characterize not one but many eupraxiae. In short, Ames is reaffirming the essential unity of art and eupraxia in the mind and exercise of God, even though man perceives and delineates God's wisdom as fragmented and through many acts of arts.

Thesis 38. Ames sets forth several alternative ways of speaking about the delineations that clearly and accurately represent the idea of eupraxia. Ames defines an "axiom" in *Demonstratio Logicae Verae,* theses 76–77, pp. 141–42. He has explained above, in theses 3 and 4, what he means by that which "rules" the following eupraxia. The description of these delineations as "precepts" because they rule by commanding, like the edicts of magistrates, reveals how closely Ames's voluntarist understanding of rule and law is connected with that of a sovereign's command: "A law is made by commanding and forbidding. A law is established by promising and threatening" (*Marrow of Theology,* bk. 1, chap. 10, theses 6–7, p. 111). In calling the delineations of the idea of eupraxia "phenomena," Ames is stressing that the prattomena of the various arts "appear" in them.

Thesis 39. Ames prefers to call the delineations of the idea of eupraxia "rules" (*regula*) because he has made the notion of "ruling" the primary essence of "idea" (theses 3–5, above) and a part of the general essence of art (thesis 12, above). Richardson prefers to call these delineations "precepts" (*praecepta*); see *The Logicians School-Master*, pp. 21–22.

Thesis 40. Ames sets forth his definition of "universal," which means "most true, most just, and most wise." Cf. Richardson, *The Logicians School-Master*, pp. 15–16, in light of Ames's argument that the rules of art must be "universal" in this sense because they were at first in the most true, most just, and most wise God. These "universal" rules that are applicable to the precepts of art are derived from the Ramist logic, which in turn derived them from a discussion in Aristotle about the universal and necessarily true premises from which demonstrative knowledge proceeds (*Posterior Analytics* 1.3, pp. 42–43). Ramus refers to these three laws as *de omni, per se,* and *universaliter primum* (in French *"du tout," "par soi,"* and *"universal premièrement"*), which are translations of the Greek κατὰ παντὸς, καθ᾽ αὑτὸ, and καθ᾽ ὅλου πρῶτον. Ramists writing in English called these three rules or laws "the law of truth," "the law of justice," and "the law of wisdom," and Ramists writing in Latin called them "lex veritatis," "lex justitiae," and "lex sapientiae." These three universal rules or laws were at the very heart of the Ramist reform of the liberal arts: "For the laws forming art (κὰτα παντὸς, καθ᾽ αὑτὸ, καθ᾽ ὅλου πρῶτον) are common to all the arts, and likewise demand that general, homogeneous, and proper precepts be abstracted from singular things" (Ramus, *Scholarum Mathematicarum Libri unus et trigenta* [Basel, 1569], p. 114). The rest of the first major section of Ames's treatise on technometry (theses 41–87) is concerned with the meaning and implications of these three universal rules and their relation to the other (less) universal rules of art. It should be noted that a fourth law, that of prudence, is added to the other three in the discussion in theses 84–87.

Thesis 41. The "universality" of the rules of art implies their eternity, unchangeability, necessity, certainty, and infallibility. These rules cannot, therefore, be true only in part, that is, doubtful. This concept of partial or doubtful truth is identical with

Ames's teaching about "opinion"; see *Disputatio Repetita, & Vindicata de Fidei Divinae Veritate,* bound after *Medulla Theologica* (Amsterdam, 1648), 1:357; also *Demonstratio Logicae Verae,* thesis 80, pp. 142–43. Ames's approval of those who derive "art" (*ars*) from "tower" (*arx*) should be compared with *Alia Technometriae Delineatio,* thesis 15, p. 47, where he approvingly adds the alternative derivation from "sinew" (*artus*), "because just as the sinews are the strength of the body, so the precepts of the arts preserve and integrate art"; cf. Richardson, *The Logicians School-Master,* p. 18.

Thesis 42. Ames begins his discussion of the first rule or law according to which the universal rules that delineate art as the idea of eupraxia come into being. This discussion continues from thesis 42 through the peroration on truth in thesis 77. Ames sets forth all that he understands and means by "truth" within the compass of these thesis. The first rule is the law of truth, κατὰ παντὸς, which Aristotle defines as follows: "I apply the term 'predicated of all' (κατὰ παντὸς) to whatever is *not* predicated of one instance but not of another, or predicated at one time but not at another" (*Posterior Analytics* 1:4, pp. 42–43). This so-called "first law" indicates in Aristotle that the predicate of a strictly scientific proposition must be true of every case of the subject. Ramus, applying this law to the axioms of art, sifted out of the liberal arts any propositions that were true only at times, that is, such propositions that were in the field of opinion rather than science; see *La Dialectique de M. Pierre de La Ramée* (Paris, 1576), fol. 38v–39r. Ames's use of this first rule or law in thesis 42 reflects both the Aristotelian usage (that is, the consequent must be true about the whole antecedent) and the Ramist interest in all the principles of art being harmonious with this law of truth. The word "principles" (*principia*) is identical with the Greek ἀρχαί, "first principles" or "first causes" of things." Ames is thinking in thesis 42 of "rules" as logical propositions or axioms, and the "principles" of these rules are the "individual arguments" or "first principles" out of which the rules are axiomatically composed. The derivation of thesis 42 from Ramist logic is confirmed elsewhere by Ames's logical interpretation of the law of truth, which takes place in the context of a discussion of *necessary axioms;* see *Demonstratio Logicae Verae,* thesis 83, p. 143.

Thesis 43. For Ames, understanding is the first thing that is required for art: "The following are required for art: understanding [*intellectus*] of the principles which are necessary to the thing; science [*scientia*] of the principles to be joined among themselves; deduction of some things from others through wisdom [*sapientia*]; prudence [*prudentia*] with regard to the use of all things to be applied; and the execution itself which is properly called art [*ars*]; and if art be transmitted from one to another, it is called teaching [*doctrina*] or discipline [*disciplina*]" (Prologomena to *Demonstratio Logicae Verae,* thesis 2, p. 121. Understanding (*intelligentia*) is taught in thesis 43 as a part of the first universal rule of art, namely, the law of truth. Knowledge (*scientia*) is treated in thesis 79 in the context of knowing the principles that have been homogeneously composed according to the second universal rule, the law of justice. Wisdom (*sapientia*) is taught in thesis 80, where truly and homogeneously composed principles are also reciprocally distributed according to the third universal rule, the law of wisdom. And finally, prudence (*prudentia*) is treated in thesis 84 as the methodical ordering according to the law of prudence or method of those principles that have been understood, homogeneously composed, and reciprocally distributed. Prudence, together with the other three universal rules, renders art complete. It should be noted that Ames is again involved in Aristotle's description of the five qualities through which the mind achieves truth; see *Nichomachean Ethics* 6.3.1, pp. 330–33. Ames's understanding of these terms differs from that of Aristotle insofar as he understands them all as various modes of one and the same genus, namely, art.

Thesis 44. Ames draws a distinction between God's archetypal understanding of the principles of art and man's derivative, imitative, refracted (that is, "ectypal") understanding. He explains God's archetypal understanding of the principles of things in thesis 45, and he explains man's ectypal understanding in thesis 47.

Thesis 45. Ames again grounds the arts in God by placing the principles of all things in divine understanding. He again stresses the unity of art and of all the principles of art in the mind and exercise of God, as over against the refracted multiplicity of the principles of created things and of man's understanding (cf. theses 15 and 37, above; also *Marrow of Theology* bk. 1, chap. 7, theses 14–17, 19–20, 22, 29, pp. 95–97). There is a strong Neoplatonic cast to thesis 45, especially in his discussion about the light shining in and around the "type"; the Latin word *"typus"* means "the mark of a blow," and hence a "stamp," "impression," "print," or "mark." Ames is asserting that God's own understanding is, though in a broken or refracted way, really "impressed" or "stamped" on the things created and governed by Him. And it is from this "type" of divine understanding impressed on things that man's own understanding of the principles of things is derived.

Thesis 46. Ames again uses language that betrays a powerful Neoplatonic bias. He is certainly using "theology" in a much more general, "archetypal" sense than he does in his definition of the "ectypal" art or teaching of theology in thesis 110, below. Ames makes no attempt, in thesis 46 or elsewhere in his writings, to identify the divine wisdom or understanding with his Christology. Yet the similarity of language between Ames and the Renaissance Platonists, who did make such an identification, remains striking in this thesis.

Thesis 47. Ames has described God's archetypal understanding of art. He now turns to describing man's ectypal understanding of art. After man has invented and understood the principles of art, his artistic activity is, by imitation of the archetypal art of God, the cause and principle of some further type of created things. But man's understanding of the divine wisdom stamped upon created things is only a faint copy of the original divine understanding. Since the wisdom or understanding of God stamped upon things must first be learned and broken down by analysis before it can be imitated by genesis, man's understanding is most different from God's. Man's ectypal understanding is drawn from the entypal understanding in things and the ectypal understanding in man. And since man's art is imitative, it always takes some entypal understanding (that is, the principles of art in created things) as its beginning point.

For an example of how this distinction between God's archetypal understanding, the entypal understanding in created things, and the derivative, ectypal understanding in man leads to the Ramist doctrine of "the manifoldness of truth," see George Downame, *In Petri Rami . . . Dialecticam Commentarii,* pp. 496–97.

Thesis 48. In spite of the enormous gap depicted in thesis 47 between God's archetypal and man's ectypal understanding, Ames states in thesis 48 that man in his own artistic activity imitates the creative activity of God the Creator and Governor. This is an extremely lofty and exalted view both of man's powers and his activities.

Thesis 49. The derivation of the Greek word for "art," τέχνη, from τεύχομαι is apparently a defective etymology from the Greek verb τεύχω, which means "produce by work or art" and refers especially to making or building material things. The Latin *"fabrico,"* used to translate the Greek verb τεύχομαι, means "to make," "frame," "form," or "construct." Τέχνη and τεύχομαι are related to the nouns τεύχημα, "fabric," and τεύχος, which not only can be used to refer to tools and instruments but also can be used in a medical sense to mean "the human frame or body." Richardson also utilizes the derivation of τέχνη from τεύχομαι and *fabrico,* and he uses the word "frame" in a way that parallels Ames's use of "type"; see *The Logicians School-Master,* pp. 18–19.

Thesis 50. This thesis shows how, in spite of the protest against metaphysics, technometry takes the place of and functions as the discipline of metaphysics in Ames's thought. Metaphysics is traditionally understood as the science of being as such (*entis qua entis*) and of being's transcendental principles, that is, of the principles common to God, stones, trees, men, etc. Thesis 50 deals with the identical problems in the same kind of language as did the more traditional metaphysics. This tendency is even more pronounced in Richardson, who begins his Preface to *The Logicians School-Master* with a discussion of being (*ens*); see pp. 1–2, 7. These ontological discussions of Ames and Richardson are really abstractions from the subject matter dealt with by the individual arts, especially by the arts of logic and theology. Nevertheless, it is also true that Ames wants to "ground the principles of art" in the preliminary discipline of technometry. And after he has abstracted the foundation of the arts in being, his thought then moves forward again from the metacritical, technological point of view to establish the norms and exercise of all the individual arts. When Ames speaks in thesis 50 about "the being of pure reason or of the one remaining insofar as it is and exists in reason alone or in the understanding of someone," it might sound as if he were expressing some form of idealism where "to be is to be perceived." But Ames is insistent that "sense perception does not perceive universals but individuals" ("Theses Physiologicae," chap. 45, thesis 1, p. 48). Furthermore, "individuals are perceived first and more easily by the intellect than universals," although he goes on to say that "the reason of the order in perception and in the accurate transmission of the disciplines is clearly contrary" (ibid., chap. 55, theses 11 and 13, p. 52); cf. *The Logicians School-Master,* pp. 218–19. Ames's final appellation of being "which is not so that it ought to have been" as "privative non-being" parallels Richardson's premise that being (*ens*) and good (*bonum*) are all one (*The Logicians School-Master,* p. 2). This fusion of the ontological and the ethical or moral reflects the Neoplatonic and Augustinian emphasis on the ultimate unity of the Beautiful, the True, and the Good, where evil is always treated not as an entity in itself but rather as a lack of being.

Thesis 51. Ames unleashes his vehemence and sarcasm against the Aristotelian and scholastic science of metaphysics. Ames inherited much of this distaste for metaphysics from Ramus, who had voiced a similar attack; see *Scholarum Metaphysicarum Liber I,* in *Scholae in Liberales Artes,* col. 829. It is not only that metaphysics usurps much that belongs to logic but also that it executes a culpable and dangerous usurpation of the subject matter that ought to be transmitted by the art of theology (ibid., col. 996). Ames's (or Peter Brest's) *Adversus Metaphysicam* picks up these same two major emphases of Ramus's critique, namely, that metaphysics usurps the tasks of logic and theology (thesis 5, p. 87). Ames's theological critique of metaphysics is further elaborated and elucidated in thesis 112, below. In thesis 51 he launches into a more logical attack on metaphysics for breaking the second Ramist law of justice, which, although treated specifically in logic, ultimately applies to the rules of all art. In assuming the task of assigning names or appellations to created things insofar as they are beings (namely, the names or appellations listed above in thesis 50), metaphysics illegitimately usurps the task of other arts. For example, the task of preparing etymological lexicons or dictionaries is one of the uses or faculties of the art of grammar, and the task of preparing logical or general philosophical lexicons is one of the uses or faculties of logic. Alsted's discussion of the "art" of *lexica* is illuminating for Ames's mention of etymological and logical or general philosophical lexicons. Alsted makes *lexica* the first of the four poetic, liberal arts, which also include grammar, rhetoric, and logic; see *Sciagraphia Encyclopaediae,* Table 6, in *Encyclopaedia,* before vol. 1, p. 6. He defines "lexica" as "the art concerning the signification of words." He speaks not only of dictionaries of the various languages but also of the various disciplines. Ames differs from Alsted insofar as he does not understand the "making well" of the various dictionaries to be the essence of any individual art; rather, the various arts would lead through their use or exercise to the production of such dictionaries.

Thesis 52. Ames has argued in thesis 51 that if metaphysics claims responsibility for giving names to things insofar as they are, it falls upon Charybdis insofar as it usurps the subject matter of etymological or logical lexicons. He argues in thesis 52 that if metaphysics claims responsibility for giving the reasons for the names or appellations of things, it falls upon Scylla insofar as it usurps the subject matter of the art of logic. This same general argument is set forth in *Adversus Metaphysicam,* thesis 8, p. 91; also theses 15 and 17, pp. 95 and 96.

Thesis 53. Ames sets forth a list of appellations assigned to beings by logic. The first three in the list (namely, that "some being is one, true, and good") are the three so-called "transcendental principles" common to all being in the Aristotelian-scholastic science of metaphysics; cf. *Adversus Metaphysicam,* theses 9, 10, p. 92. The distribution of logic into the two parts of invention and disposition (judgment) is examined below in the commentary on thesis 98. Ames elaborates in thesis 56 and following what he means by "the affections of things."

Thesis 54. Ames has argued above that logic gives appellations to created things insofar as they are beings. Such responsibility includes the task of *defining* the nature or essence of things. But such logical consideration of the nature of things is both different from and more abstract than the physical consideration of nature, or, more accurately, the general art of logic is only concerned with setting forth the *general essence* or nature of things insofar as they are beings and not their *whole nature,* which is made up of *form and matter.* For Ramists, nature arises from the act of form upon matter, and that form is the principle nature of things (see Richardson, *The Logicians School-Master,* p. 229). Physics, as a posterior and special art, uses the eupraxia and rules of logic, which is a prior and general art. This means that physics presupposes the logical definitions and the logical reasons for the names of created things, but it is also concerned with the substance and properties of all individual, existing things. Ames argues that this is the task of physics on the basis of what he has said above concerning the resolution of being insofar as it is the type of art (theses 45–50), and he says that this will become clearer in thesis 55 and following, where being is further resolved insofar as it is the type of art.

Thesis 55. Ames has already said in thesis 48 that "type . . . is primarily things created and governed by God, but secondarily made or produced in a similar manner by man." The principles of art first appear and shine forth *around* the type and then *in it.* The arts that are grounded in the principles appearing and shining forth *around* the type are dealt with in theses 56 and 57 (that is, the principles of the general arts of dialectic, grammar, and rhetoric). These arts, which are grounded in the principles appearing and shining forth *in* the type, are dealt with in theses 58, 59, and 60 (that is, the principles of the special arts of mathematics, physics, and theology).

Thesis 56. For both Ames and Richardson, logic is primarily the act by which the reason, relation, and mutual affection of things are transmitted from the things themselves to man's "eye" of logic or reason. The "reason," "relation," "affection," and "argument" of things all mean the same thing for Ames and are interchangeable terms. It should be noted that Ames does not confuse "the affection [*affectio*] of things" with "the affects [*affectus*]" or "emotions" of men (see "Theses Physiologicae," chap. 52, theses 9, 10, p. 50). While Ames speaks about the reason, relation, and the mutual affection of things shining forth around the type everywhere and from its every part, Richardson prefers to speak of the reason and affection of things as shining forth "around being" (*The Logicians School-Master*, pp. 33–34).

Thesis 57. If the self-propelled conveyance of the reason, relation, and mutual affection of things to the "eye" of man's reason is the source of the principles of discoursing (that is, of logic), the similarly but subordinately self-propelled conveyance of the names or appellations of things is the source of the principles of speaking and communicating (that is, of grammar and rhetoric).

Thesis 58. Ames turns to the sources of the special arts *in* the type, namely, the principles of mathematics in thesis 58, of physics in thesis 59, and of theology in thesis 60. When Ames says that quantity is the first thing to be seen in type because all things are *first* made from matter, he is reflecting the Ramist teaching that efficient and material causes are prior in order and nature to formal and final causes; cf. *Demonstratio Logicae Verae*, theses 11, 12, pp. 126–27. Ames presupposes that all created things, including angels, have matter and are thus to be distinguished from God the Creator, who is, among his other attributes, immaterial. And since all created things have matter, they have quantity, magnitude, or extension, which is subject to measurement (geometry) and numbering (arithmetic).

Thesis 59. It has been pointed out above, in the commentary on thesis 54, that although matter is part of the essence or nature of a thing, form is the principal nature of things (cf. *Demonstratio Logicae Verae*, theses 17–18, p. 128.) Ames's emphasis on "the principal form, which is the particular nature of things," means that there can be more than one form in a composite, but it is the highest or most noble form that makes up the essential nature of a thing; cf. "Theses Physiologicae," chap. 40, thesis 6, p. 46. The natures, especially the principal forms seen in the type of things, are the source of the principles of the art of physics (that is, of doing the work of nature well).

Thesis 60. The third thing seen in the type is the end or final cause; cf. Ames's discussion of final cause in *Demonstratio Logicae Verae,* theses 19–20, pp. 128–29. Although the end or final cause is last in order, it is that toward which all the other principles appearing and shining *around* and *in* the type of things are oriented. Goodness or perfection is not only the end of all nature (that is, the inner principle of action or motion) but is also the end or scope of God the Creator and Governor of all things. When Ames declares that the end seen in the type of things is "the glory of God," he places himself squarely within the mainstream of Calvinists who not only ordered their theology but also saw all things in the light of and for the sake of God's glory. This emphasis upon God's glory does not, however, annihilate or exclude human happiness from a legitimate role in theology. For Ames, man's happiness is always a subordinate chief end along with the universal chief end, namely, God's glory (*Marrow of Theology,* bk. 2, chap. 1, theses 27–29, pp. 228–29; also *Conscience,* bk. 2, chap. 14, thesis 13, p. 34). What is true for theology as *living well* or *living to God* is true for all the other arts that *practice well,* namely, insofar as any or all of them are *well* taught, learned, and executed, they discern and manifest the wisdom and glory of God in the things that he has created. Ames's quotation from Marsilio Ficino (1433–99), the Florentine Renaissance Platonist, is taken slightly out of context, for Ficino is speaking here specifically of Plato and not of just anyone in general; see Ficino, *Prooemium in Platonicam Theologiam,* in *Opera Omnia* (Turin: Bottega d'Erasmo, 1962), 1:78. Ficino may well have been one of the Renaissance Platonist sources for the Neoplatonic elements that come so strikingly to view at various places in the *Technometry;* see the commentary on thesis 45, above.

Thesis 61. Ames explains the obscurity and difficulty of discerning the principles of art shining around and in the type of created things in terms of the Christian doctrine of original sin. It is important to note that man's fall into sin led to an obscuration and corruption *primarily* of the principles of goodness that are communicated *in* the types of things. The remaining principles, which are the sources of dialectic, grammar, rhetoric, mathematics, and physics, are *relatively* unimpaired (see thesis 66, below). Nevertheless, Ames is insistent that sin is a corruption of the *whole* man (that is, his understanding, conscience, will, affections, and body; see *Marrow of Theology,* bk. 1, chap. 13, thesis 4, p. 120). Ames argues that even though sin obscures and corrupts the powers or faculties of the *whole* man, the principles of conscience shining in the synteresis of man have been the most obscured and corrupted of all. Ames's statement that the remaining creatures have been subjected to a curse and vanity because of man's sin reflects the biblical theme that the ground is cursed because of Adam's sin (Gen. 3:17 ff.) and that the whole creation groans in travail until the redemption of men is accomplished (Rom. 8:22–23).

Thesis 62. Ames moderates the implications of thesis 61 by emphasizing that, due to God's mercy, man has not been left totally in the dark, even with regard to principles and matters of conscience; cf. *Marrow of Theology,* bk. 1, chap. 14, theses 21–28, pp. 123–24. Ames believes with Calvin that the basic principles of conscience (or, more narrowly and specifically, synteresis) are "vanishing and dead" and hence serve to condemn man rather than to save him; but he also follows Calvin in asserting that the shadows of virtues are recognized and embraced by all. From the obscured and corrupted but still remaining principles of goodness that shine in man's synteresis, Ames derives his theory of "natural conscience" (*Conscience,* bk. 1, chap. 2, thesis 5, p. 4), upon which he develops a relatively optimistic yet realistic social theory. But the natural or "darkened" conscience fades into insignificance in comparison with the "enlightened" conscience illuminated by the merciful new revelation of God's will in the Holy Scriptures; see *Conscience,* bk. 1, chap. 2, theses 6–8, pp. 4–5. These principles of goodness, which are darkly and corruptly visible in the type of things and in man's apprehension of those principles, are thus perfectly and sufficiently apprehended by means of God's revealed will, that is, by means of the Holy Scriptures. By declaring that the Scriptures most perfectly reveal the principles of goodness, he is affirming the Reformation principle of the perfection and all-sufficiency of Scripture; cf. Ames's fourth treatise in *Philosophemata,* entitled *A Theological Disputation concerning the Perfection of Holy Scripture.* . . .

Thesis 63. Ames launches his attack against the ethicists or moral philosophers. It has been pointed out in the commentary on thesis 34, and Ames demonstrates below in theses 88–94, that he rejects the distinction between theoretical and practical philosophy. Moreover, since the Scriptures sufficiently and perfectly reveal the principles of goodness and virtue, and since theology *alone* transmits the whole revealed will of God for directing man's morals, will, and life, there is no longer any need for a separate discipline, science, or art of ethics. The distinction that the ethicists make on the basis of their primary distinction between natural ethics and supernatural theology are distinctions that are outlined and rejected by Ames in thesis 116, below. The attack on practical philosophy or natural ethics is one of the central themes of his treatise *Adversus Ethicam* in *Philosophemata;* see esp. *Adversus Ethicam,* thesis 18, p. 108; thesis 24, p. 112. Just as Ames derived much of his vehement distaste for metaphysics from Ramus, so also did he derive from Ramus a strong distaste for natural ethics; see, for example, *Marrow of Theology,* bk. 2, chap. 2, thesis 18, pp. 226–27, where Ames gives hearty approval to an anti-Aristotelian passage from Ramus's *Pro Philosophica Parisiensis Academics discipline oratio,* in *Collectaneae,* p. 337.

Thesis 64. In theses 64 and 65 Ames utilizes a time-honored device of Jewish and Christian apology, namely, the appeal to antiquity for originality and authority. Whatever "histories" Ames is referring to here, they undoubtedly reflect this early Judaeo-Christian argument about the antiquity (and thereby authority) of the divine revelation in the Hebrew Scriptures. He presupposes this argument below in thesis 115, where he goes on to argue the imperfection of ethics and its "borrowing of principles" from theology.

Thesis 65. Ames is concerned in theses 64 and 65 with the apparent virtue or goodness expressed in the lives and writings of many pagans who stood outside Christian faith and the Church. Ames holds that without faith, Christ, and grace there is no true virtue, holiness, or righteousness. He is therefore in essential agreement with the Augustinian-Calvinist interpretation of the virtues of the pagans as "splendid vices." But Ames also sees many praiseworthy vestiges of the principles of goodness in the writings of the pagans, and hence he admits that they may legitimately be read and analyzed by Christians. Nevertheless, they must always be subordinated to and tested by the Holy Scriptures—the only, perfect, and sufficient rule, law, or canon of life and morals. In light of the Scriptures, such "vestiges of honesty" as remain in pagan writers appear very faint and most inferior. It is from the unlimited teaching examples of all predicable virtues contained in the Scriptures, and not from those inferior, corrupted, and imitated examples of the pagans, that the precepts of Christian imitation are to be constituted; see *Adversus Ethicam,* thesis 16 ff., pp. 113 ff.

Thesis 66. Ames argues that since man's fall into sin the principles of art shining around and in the type of created things may (with the exception of goodness) still be gathered in their inner essence by the slow, painful, steady process of analysis. The cautious optimism and somber realism of Ames's position is also that of Francis Bacon, whom Ames mentions below in thesis 70; see Bacon, *Novum Organum,* bk. 2, chap. 52, in *The Works of Francis Bacon* (Boston, 1861), 1:538–39.

Thesis 67. The transition from thesis 66 to 67 is awkward, for Ames moves abruptly from a thesis about the remaining principles still adequately conveyed by type back to a discussion of the principles of goodness revealed in Scripture. The common middle term or fulcrum between the two theses is "analysis." Thesis 67 is of immense importance for correctly understanding Ames's conception of the relation between logic and theology and for correcting any overemphasis upon Ames's theological voluntarism to the exclusion of all intellectual elements of faith. Ames is not concerned in this thesis with faith as an electing act of the *will* (that is, of the *whole* man); rather, he is concerned with *understanding* the principles of goodness revealed in Scripture, both by means of analysis and by means of the supernatural enlightening of the eyes of the mind by the Holy Spirit. Ames wrote a short treatise dealing with the content of thesis 67, namely, *Assertiones Theologica de Lumine Naturae et Gratiae.* The major problem under consideration in this treatise is whether and how far man in his natural state, destitute of special illumination and grace, can understand from the Scriptures the things that are necessary to salvation in faith and action. Ames stresses that the logical, grammatical, and rhetorical analysis of Scripture *precedes* the opening of the eyes of the mind by the Holy Spirit. But the intellectual understanding of and assent to the truths and principles of goodness in the Scriptures are not *real* until the eyes of the mind have been opened by the supernatural light bestowed by the Holy Spirit.

Thesis 68. In *Alia Technometriae Delineatio* (thesis 62, p. 60), Ames treats the content of thesis 68 in a wider context: "How is the analysis of Holy Scriptures and of things accomplished?" In thesis 68 Ames is isolating "the analysis of Scripture" in terms of the principles of logic rightly applied so that he may isolate "the analysis of things" in thesis 69. Although grammar and rhetoric are also used in the analysis of Scripture, they are subordinate to, or handmaidens serving, the most general art of logic. Although logic is, as the most general art, complete and independent from the most special art of theology, its most dignified or important use is nevertheless the proper analysis of Holy Scripture. By means of logic, the arguments that make up the precepts of faith and morals are to be invented or discovered, and then they are to be ordered by logical method. The necessary priority of logic is again affirmed in thesis 68, as it was above in theses 24 and 67 and as it is below in thesis 120.

Thesis 69. Ames lays out the process of analysis in terms of the four "helps" that are necessary for gathering the most true principles of all the liberal arts. Ames's explication of this process sets forth his theory as to how man moves from sense impressions through observation and induction to the most true principles of the arts, and finally to the testing and confirmation of these principles by experience. The four steps and the terms used to define them have a long philosophical tradition behind them, a tradition that once again may be traced back to Aristotle; see *Posterior Analytics* 2.19, pp. 256–61; also Ramus, *Rami in Agrarias Praefatio,* in *Collectaneae,* p. 143. Ames asserts that appearances and perceptibles (that is, the things themselves or their effects) are immediately apprehended by sense perception; to this extent he is following Aristotle. He only appears to depart from Aristotle when he comes to the second level of analysis, namely, observation ($\iota\sigma\tau o\rho\iota\alpha$). Aristotle holds that sense perception gives rise to memory, which in turn gives rise to experience. Ames, however, says that analysis is carried forward by $\iota\sigma\tau o\rho\iota\alpha$, which he translates by "observation." The Greek noun $\iota\sigma\tau o\rho\iota\alpha$ basically means "inquiry" or "investigation," but it can also mean "systematic or scientific observation" or "the knowledge or information so obtained," and hence, finally, "a written account of one's inquiries." Ames's emphasis on the fact that observation *carefully knows and retains* those things that have been perceived by sense perception shows that he is interested in a systematic observation and perhaps retaining the result of such systematic observation in the memory. This position is not in any basic disagreement with Aristotle, who claims that sense perception gives rise to memory. Ames's concept of induction as the third step in analysis is essentially that of Aristotle, for whom induction is the progress from particulars to universals. Ames uses "experience" not so much as a part of the process of analysis as a final judge or arbiter that tests the validity or truth of the universal principles. Experience performs this function by carefully examining and testing the validity of the inductive reasoning from individuals and by constantly checking the universal principles against further sense perceptions and observations given on various occasions. It is quite evident that there is a strong tendency toward both induction and empiricism in this thesis, a tendency that becomes even more pronounced in theses 70 and 72.

Thesis 70. Ames states that the investigations (that is, $\iota\sigma\tau o\rho\iota\alpha\iota$ in the sense discussed above in the commentary on thesis 69) of all the individual arts are to be carried on by means of the four "helps" or parts of analysis enumerated in thesis 69. The distinction between notational or observational investigations on the one hand and inductive or experimental investigations on the other rests upon the language of Francis Bacon (1561–1626) in *The Advancement of Learning,* in his *Novum Organum,* and in *The Natural and Experimental History, for the Making Up of Philosophy, or, Experiments of the Universe.* Verulamius is the Latin name used for Bacon, whose full title was Baron of Verulam,

Viscount of St. Alban, and Lord High Chancellor of England. Bacon's talk about a "natural" and "experimental" history or investigation corresponds, Ames thinks, with the distinction between observation (ἱστορία) and induction (ἐπαγωγή) in thesis 69, of *Technometry*. Bacon does indeed speak of and later attempted the beginnings of a natural and experimental history to serve as a foundation for philosophy; see Bacon, *Novum Organum,* bk. 2, chap. 10, in *The Works of Francis Bacon* (Boston, 1861), 1:353–54. The problem with Ames's appeal to Bacon here, as well as his appeal to Pliny's *Natural History* (ἱστορία) and Aristotle's *Historia Animalium,* is that all of these works are primarily oriented toward and concerned with the natural world and natural philosophy, that is, what was then called "physics." Yet Ames is appealing to these authors as examples of how the most true first principles of *all* the individual arts (including logic, grammar, and rhetoric) should be apprehended by analysis. The point of connection between these two different views is that Ames finds the principles of all the arts shining around and in created things, which calls for analysis of the creatures in order that these principles might be known by man. Ames appeals to Bacon, Pliny, and Aristotle, for he believes that both their mode of approaching their investigations and also the results of their investigations are useful for constituting, understanding, and correcting all the disciplines or arts—provided, that is, they are not made dictatorial authorities who exclude or cut off knowledge from other or new investigations. This danger was especially great in the case of Aristotle, as the last statement of thesis 70 makes clear. In conclusion, it may be affirmed that Ames strengthened the tendencies of Ramus toward empiricism, observation, and experiment, at least in the discovery of the principles of various disciplines. And if Ramus was a transitional figure between the old, authoritative, scholastic understanding of the arts and the new philosophy of Descartes and the new science of Bacon, Boyle, and Newton, Ames certainly progressed farther down the road of transition than did his master. Ames, with his influence in England, on the continent, and especially in early New England, not only helped clear the way for but actually helped introduce the new science.

Thesis 71. Ames begins in this thesis to draw a series of conclusions from his discussion of the rules of art as being most true if their principles are harmonious with the laws of truth (theses 42–70). The first conclusion is drawn in thesis 71 and elaborated in thesis 72; the second conclusion is drawn in thesis 73; the third in thesis 74; the fourth in thesis 75; and the fifth in thesis 76. The first conclusion that Ames draws from his discussion of analysis is that the neglect of one or more of the four steps in analysis, which are necessary for gathering the most true principles of the individual arts, is the major source of all the errors, defects, and controversies in the individual arts.

Thesis 72. Ames expresses his conviction that among the four helps, the neglect of analysis is greatest and has the most devastating consequences for the knowledge and practice of the art of physics. The cynical observation that scarcely any of the subject matter of physics is free from faults should be compared with the last part of thesis 31, where he says that the eupraxia of physics (that is, doing the work of nature well) has been united with more imperfection than can be found in any other eupraxia —except in the eupraxia of theology (that is, in living well). In thesis 72 Ames partially explains why physics was among the two weakest and most imperfect of all the arts by directing two basic criticisms at the transmission and practice of the art of physics, both in the past and in his own day. First, physicists did not make experiments of natural things whereby they might gather the truer principles of physics or test and correct those principles that had been previously gathered. And secondly, physicists have remained submissive to former physicists (especially to Aristotle) by taking the writings and discoveries of the ancients as authoritative and by being willing merely to catalogue and classify the results of previous investigations. Ames expresses his antiauthoritarianism with a rhetorical flourish by calling physicists who are bound to the past "mystagogues" (that is, high priests of the pagan mystery cults) who superstitiously worship the writings of certain ancients and regard innovations or any departures from these writings as "sacrilege." This criticism of servile submission to the authority of the past, which is also essential to the arguments of theses 73, 74, and 77, was also a part of Bacon's removal of the impediments facing natural philosophy; see Bacon, *Novum Organum,* bk. 1, chap. 84, in *The Works of Francis Bacon,* 1:291.

Thesis 73. Ames grants cautious approval, honor, and respect to the writings of the wise and learned ancients. Whatever principles the ancients have gathered from the analysis of things are to be used by the individual arts. But, he says, the writings that record the results of the investigations of the ancients should be constantly tested and corrected by the further analysis of things and experiments. The cautious optimism expressed in the conviction that modern writers on the whole know more and more clearly than the ancients is in essential agreement with Bacon's paradox, "antiquitas saeculi, juventus mundi" (*Novum Organum,* bk. 1, chap. 84, in *The Works of Francis Bacon,* 1:290–91).

Thesis 74. In this thesis Ames is referring back to what he has said in theses 64 and 65 about the pagan imitation of the true virtue revealed in the Scriptures of the Hebrews. To the extent that there are vestiges of virtue in their writings, their writings are to be read, praised, and honored by Christians. But since these vestiges are really only spiritually dead images of the principles of virtue revealed in the Scriptures and originated and nourished by God in the saints, the writings are to be subordinated to and tested by the Scriptures, the only rule and canon of faith and morals. Furthermore, on the basis of what he has set forth in thesis 67 about the opening of the eyes of the mind by the Holy Spirit so that the Christian may understand the real or spiritual meaning of the principles of goodness revealed in the Scriptures, he can conclude that, other things being equal, the writings of Christians are to be preferred to those of pagans.

Thesis 75. Ames introduces in this thesis a new dimension to his previous discussion of the means whereby the most true principles of the arts are to be gathered, whether by untiring analysis or (with the aid of the Holy Spirit) by the principles of goodness made known again in the revelation in the Holy Scriptures. This new dimension is "a sincere love of truth" and "uprightness of life," that is, the moral dimension of the will; see Ames, *The*

Substance of the Christian Religion, p. 258. This moral dimension of truth presupposes a work of the Spirit beyond that of the illumination of the mind; see *Adversus Ethicam,* thesis 22, pp. 110–11. The distinction to be made between Christian writers is not so much to be based upon the accurateness and intellectual validity of the principles of the arts (especially the principles of goodness) that they transmit in their writings as upon the moral intention of the writer and the moral uprightness of his life. This thesis clearly manifests Ames's basic conviction that it is not enough for Christians to be orthodox in thought or understanding alone; they must also be orthodox or upright in their hearts, will, and life.

Thesis 76. Ames has stated in theses 63 and 65 that the Scriptures are the only rule or canon for living well or living to God. And since it is the nature of a rule or canon to be neither added to nor subtracted from, the opinions of men (Christians or pagans) can add nothing to the revelation of God's will or law in the Scriptures. Nevertheless, since the eyes of Christians have been opened by the revelation of Scripture and by the accompanying supernatural illumination of the Holy Spirit, the opinions of Christians about theological matters are to be preferred over those of pagans. Ames's preference for the opinions or judgments of Christians in the realm of jurisprudence rests upon his conviction that jurisprudence is almost totally dependent upon theology for its principles; see *Marrow of Theology,* bk. 1, chap. 1, thesis 12, p. 78. This position is worked out much more fully in theses 113–16, below.

Thesis 77. This is the rhetorical peroration that concludes Ames's discussion of the most true principles that make up the rules of the arts. For Ames, the "elders" or "the ancients" are only men created in the (fallen) image of Adam; this means that their authority or testimony is only human, not divine, and is therefore open to error or hallucinations. All things are to be tested constantly (by the four steps of the analysis of things and by experiments), appropriated for oneself, and retained insofar as they are true or good. The final quotation with which Ames concludes thesis 77 has a long and complex tradition behind it. It is grounded in and attributed to a passage in Aristotle: "Still perhaps it would appear desirable, and indeed it would seem to be obligatory, especially for a philosopher, to sacrifice even one's closest personal ties in defence of the truth. Both are dear to us, yet 'tis our duty to prefer the truth" (*Nichomachean Ethics* 1.6, p. 17). Ramus uses the quotation in a form almost identical to that of Ames, the only difference being that he uses the name of Socrates for that of Aristotle; see Ramus, *Scholarum Mathematicarum Lib. III*, p. 78. The quotation appeared on the title or subtitle page of every edition of Ames's *Philosophemata* (Leyden, 1643; Cambridge, 1646; Amsterdam, 1651, also bound into volume 5 of Ames's collected Latin works in the 1658 Amsterdam edition). The quotation continued to be used in New England after Ames's death; see, for example, the excerpt given by Cotton Mather from a commencement oration given by Increase Mather, who was then president of Harvard University (*Magnalia*, bk. 4, pt. 1, par. 7, 2:21). The prominence of this quotation on the title or subtitle pages of Ames's *Philosophemata* may well be the original source of Harvard's *veritas* motto; see S. E. Morison, *The Founding of Harvard College*, p. 330.

Thesis 78. Ames sets forth the second rule or law according to which the universal rules that delineate the idea of eupraxia come into being. This is the second requirement established in Ames's affirmation that the rules of the arts must be universal. The discussion of this second rule (theses 78–79) is brief in comparison with the discussion of the first (theses 42–77). This second rule is the law of justice, κατὰ τὸ αὐτὸ, per se. The second of these Aristotelian axioms, the *lex justitiae,* permitted Ramus and his followers to sift out of one liberal art any propositions that belonged to another. Ames gives his own interpretation of the law of justice in *Demonstratio Logicae Verae,* thesis 83, p. 143. What Ames is saying in thesis 78 of *Technometry* is that if the most true principles of the arts are gathered by untiring analysis from the type of things (or from Holy Scripture in the case of the principles of goodness), they become most just if they are composed or disposed homogeneously according to the law of justice. Ames is here clearly taking "justice" in its Aristotelian sense as "the virtue by means of which each thing is given its own as the law prescribes."

Thesis 79. Ames explicates the second requirement for art. The first was understanding (*intellectus*) of the principles that are necessary to the thing. The second requirement, which corresponds to the second law, the law of justice, is the science of how these principles have been joined among themselves. Ames's word "science" (*scientia*) is the Latin translation of the Platonic and Aristotelian ἐπιστήμη, "scientific knowledge." In Plato, ἐπιστήμη has to do with the eternal, immutable realm of the forms or ideas, as over against δόξα, "opinion," which has to do with the transient realm of becoming. Likewise in Aristotle, there is the emphasis that ἐπιστήμη is universal, and subsists through necessary things that cannot subsist otherwise than they do. Moreover, it is a basic thesis of his *Metaphysics* that there is scientific knowledge of things when their essences and causes are known. Furthermore, these essences and causes are ultimately "more known" than individuals. These Platonic and Aristotelian themes are sharply defined not only in Ames's use of *scientia* in thesis 79 but also elsewhere in his writings; cf. *Disputatio Repetita, et Vindicata de Fidei Divinae Veritate,* thesis 1, p. 357.

Thesis 80. This is the third rule or law according to which the universal rules that delineate art as the idea of eupraxia come into being. Ames discusses this law even more briefly than the second. The third rule, which makes up the third requirement of a "universal axiom," is called the law of wisdom, καθόλου πρῶτον, a Greek phrase that Aristotle explains in *Posterior Analytics* 1.4. In Ramus's logic an axiom that is composed according to this third law is called "reciprocal." The third of these Aristotelian axioms, the *lex sapientiae,* permitted Ramus and his followers to clarify the organization of the subject matter of the liberal arts. Ames gives his logical interpretation of the law of wisdom in *Demonstratio Logicae Verae,* theses 83, 85, pp. 143–44. When this logical interpretation is applied to the general rules of art, it means that more specific rules may be deduced from the more general ones, and insofar as the derived rules are "reciprocal," they too are "most wise." The fact that the law of wisdom, which itself presupposes the laws of truth and justice, is the logical foundation of the all important "method" of Ramus is corroborated in thesis 84, below.

Thesis 81. In thesis 39 Ames prefers to call the delineations of the idea of eupraxia "rules," while in thesis 81 he calls them "laws." He has set forth the three rules or laws that measure the universality (that is, the truth, justice, and wisdom) of the precepts of all the arts and of every individual art. Ames is quite insistent that these three aspects of a universal axiom come together only in the precepts of some art; see *Demonstratio Logicae Verae*, p. 144. These three laws must be used and carefully observed in all the disciplines or arts and in every individual discipline or art, and hence they are to be taught in this treatise concerning art in general. Ames makes one qualification, however, about how these laws are to be used and observed by all the arts and by every individual art: "These laws absolutely ought to be so observed, but disjunctively, not conjunctively, so that a later law includes a prior law, but not vice-versa" (*Alia Technometriae Delineatio*, thesis 69, p. 63). This last statement is a reassertion of the law of wisdom.

Thesis 82. The Latin word *commorationes*, "dwelling on important points," is derived from the verb *comoror*, which means "to tarry," "linger," "abide," "sojourn," "remain," or "stay." The noun means "a dwelling," "tarrying," "abiding," "lingering," or "sojourning." In rhetorical usage, *commoratio* came to mean "a delaying" or "a dwelling upon some important point"; cf. Cicero, *De Oratore*, 3.3.202, trans. H. Rackham, Loeb Classical Library (Cambridge, Mass.: Harvard University Press, 1960), 2:160–61. One of the most notable characteristics of Ames's writings is their lack of digressions and examples to clarify or amplify the points in his discussions. Ramus, in spite of his humanistic passion for conciseness and brevity, still usually gave two or three examples of each major point or division in his treatise. When Ames gives his rendition of Ramus's work (for example, in the *Demonstratio Logicae Verae*, which is often a word-for-word copying of Ramus's *Dialectica*), he simply excluded most or all of Ramus's examples or "dwellings on important points." Ames recognized that he had this passion for "concluding many things in few words" and that it led to a certain "harshness" and "dryness" of literary style; see "Briefe Premonition" to his *Marrow of Theology;* also "To the Reader," in *Conscience*, p. 1.

Thesis 83. Ames refutes the argument of those who argue that only definitions and divisions within an art are subject to the three most general laws, but not the precepts or rules of art. The persons Ames is opposing apparently argued that it is the nature or essence of a "rule" or "canon" to measure and test. Ames repeats that the general and more specific rules of all the arts are to be measured by these three most general rules common to all the arts. The three laws of truth, justice, and wisdom serve the function of measuring the legitimacy of a rule's claim to be "right" or "straight" and of testing the absolute rectitude of the rules of the arts.

Thesis 84. To this point Ames has been concerned with the definition of art in general, and he has now elaborated all aspects of the definition but one, the meaning and use of the adverb "methodically" (*methodice*). The universal axioms or rules of art, governed by the three laws discussed in theses 37–83, make up the "matter" or *material cause* of the idea of eupraxia. Eupraxia makes up the object and end (that is, the *final cause*) of art as "idea." The *efficient cause* of the art is primarily God the Creator and Governor and in a secondary and derivative sense man himself, who has to discover and organize the various individual arts. In thesis 84 Ames now turns to the form (that is, the *formal cause*) of the idea of eupraxia. The form of the idea of eupraxia is the methodical delineation of eupraxia, which produces prudence; see *Alia Technometriae Delineatio,* thesis 13, p. 47. Ames, following Ramus, holds that both invention and judgement or disposition concur toward method, just as in *Technometry* the laws of truth, justice, and wisdom concur toward or give rise to the law of method or prudence; see *Demonstratio Logicae Verae,* theses 119–120, 123–128, pp. 154–55. The intimate relationship between wisdom and prudence, as well as the inclusion of understanding and science in both, is clearly set forth in Ames's discussion of virtue in *Marrow of Theology,* bk. 2, chap. 2, theses 27–28, pp. 228–29. By adding prudence to understanding, science, and wisdom, Ames has put forward the fourth and final requirement of art. Art itself is merely the execution or putting into practice of these four prerequisites. When all of these are so executed or practiced, art is complete.

Thesis 85. Ames believes that the use or exercise of the four laws produce corresponding "habits" in the mind; see *Alia Technometriae Delineatio,* theses 12, 13, p. 47. It is at this point that hexiology becomes a part of technology or technometry (see below, thesis 119). Alsted defines hexiology as "the teaching which must be foreknown concerning intellectual habits by means of which man is disposed to understand intelligible things, that is, with respect to principles and conclusions that are put forth for the sake of cognition or action" (*Compendium Encyclopaediae Universae,* bk. 1, in *Encyclopaedia,* before Vol. 1, p. 27). In elaborating upon the content of hexiology, Alsted as usual has many more distinctions than Ames (in this case nineteen as opposed to four). Ames is aware of the fact that the four habits of the mind that he regards as necessary requirements for art are often called "intellectual virtues." He gives a very qualified acceptance of this later designation, and insofar as he accepts it, he regards such intellectual habits or virtues as "perfections of the mind"; cf. *Marrow of Theology,* bk. 2, chap. 2, thesis 27, p. 228. This discussion also recalls Ames's qualified acceptance in thesis 8, above, of the word art (*ars*) being derived from the Greek word for virtue (ἀρετή).

Thesis 86. Ames points out that even if certain ignorant persons are defective in their "theory" about the nature of and necessary requirements for art, they may still justly "practice" or produce by means of the ideas of eupraxia and the disciplines or the arts that have been properly executed and put into practice. Here is one of the consequences of the Ramist tenet that use is in nature prior to and more ancient than art or teaching; see Ramus, *Scholarum Mathematicarum Lib. III,* p. 73. Practice or use engenders the precepts or theory transmitted in the teaching of the arts. Furthermore, after nature has been improved and clarified by art, one may forget the teaching or discipline, or at least parts of it, and still adequately and justly put the precepts of the arts into practice or exercise.

Thesis 87. Ames is very severe and sarcastic with those who remove science, justice, wisdom, and prudence from the teaching or (much worse) from the practice of any discipline. Such persons consciously or unconsciously imply that the precepts of any individual art are not homogeneous (that is, they are not axioms or rules whose principles are composed according to the law of justice), are not adequate (that is, they are not general, reciprocal axioms or rules from which other less general axioms or rules may be deduced according to the law of wisdom), or do not have method (that is, they are not axioms or rules that are ordered by means of their priority in nature according to the law of method or prudence). With these two criticisms in theses 86 and 87 of those who differ with him about the four necessary requirements for art, Ames comes to the end of the first major section of his *Technometry*. In theses 1–87 he has considered the nature in general of all the arts in terms of the definition that "art is the idea of eupraxia methodically delineated by universal rules." He now turns to the second major section of his treatise.

Thesis 88. In the second major section of *Technometry*, Ames launches out into his discussion of the nature and essence of art in terms of its division (theses 88–120). He begins this discussion by giving a series of arguments against the prevalent and commonly accepted division of art into theoretical and practical (theses 88–94). The foundation for the rejection of this distinction has already been laid above in theses 10 and 32.

Thesis 89. Ames first attacks the division of arts into theoretical and practical on the grounds that the division is not based on a real or true difference, that is, a difference grounded in the nature or essence of art. What Ames means by a true or real difference is explicated below in thesis 112, where, following Duns Scotus, he says: "A real difference of knowledge cannot be the mode or respect of reason in an object; rather, a real difference must necessarily be something real." Ames is here following the medieval language of the Schools, where what we today mean by "subject" or "subjective" is expressed by "object" or "objective," and vice-versa. The point that Ames is arguing is based on the conviction that art is primarily and objectively in created things, while it is only secondarily and subjectively in human understanding. The fact that man's subjective appropriation or science (that is, scientific knowledge) of the arts may be distinguished into theoretical or practical has no bearing whatsoever on the objective reality of the arts in things; cf. Richardson, *The Logi-*

cians School-Master, p. 42. After having argued this point, Ames goes on in thesis 89 to argue that contemplation or theory and practice (with its inseparable adjunct of prattomenon or artistic work made by practical activity) are not mutually exclusive terms, or, in terms of Ramist logic, negative contraries. They are, rather, terms that mutually imply and clarify one another, that is, they are affirmative, contrary relatives; see *Demonstratio Logicae Verae,* theses 35–39, pp. 133–34.

Thesis 90. This thesis continues the argument in thesis 89. Art as theory or teaching not only is derived from nature and practice but also tends by its very nature toward practice and the making of some euprattomenon; cf. Richardson, *The Logicians School-Master,* p. 26.

Thesis 91. Ames is discussing the three arts (usually referred to as "sciences" by the Aristotelians) that were most usually taken to be purely theoretical, that is, those arts or sciences whose end is pure contemplation for its own sake. On mathematics, see thesis 28 and also the commentary on it, above; Ames considers and rejects the distinction between abstract and concrete (that is, between pure and mixed or applied) mathematics in theses 107 and 108, below. On metaphysics, cf. thesis 51 and also the commentary on it, above. Ames quotes the Apostle Paul in Romans 1:21: "For although they knew God they did not honor him as God or give any thanks to him, but they became futile in their thinking and their senseless minds were darkened." Again, in summary, Ames's attack against metaphysics is threefold. First, it usurps the responsibility of logic in assigning abstract, general names or appellations to created beings; secondly, it usurps the responsibility of theology in teaching about Infinite or First Being; and thirdly, insofar as it claims to be only or purely theoretical contemplation about God, it is vain and culpable because it does not lead to practice, that is, to living well. With regard to physics, Ames refers back to what he has said in thesis 31 about the practice or use of physics by farmers, gardeners, workmen, and many others. He also elaborates in theses 143–65 the practice or use of physics by the less dignified faculties.

Thesis 92. Ames argues against those who claim that ethics, household economy, and politics are practical sciences or arts, that is, sciences or arts concerned only with doing and action. He has argued in thesis 63 against those who, aware of the obscurity of the principles of goodness in the type of created things and of their new revelation in Holy Scriptures, nevertheless try to establish the validity of a natural, practical, or moral philosophy. In thesis 113, below, Ames argues that theology alone properly transmits the universal teaching of virtues, that is, the whole revealed will of God for directing man's morals, will, and life. He goes on to argue in thesis 128 that household economy and politics are not really "arts" or "sciences" per se but rather faculties or uses of another "art," namely, the teaching of theology. What Ames means by these faculties properly looking toward theology is explained in thesis 114. In thesis 116 he elaborates upon what he means by his adversaries wishing to move far away from theology their philosophy or arts (so divided into theoretical and practical).

Thesis 93. Ames again enters the fray against those who follow the distinction made by Aristotle between doing ($\pi\rho\hat{a}\xi\iota\varsigma$) and making ($\pi o i\eta\sigma\iota\varsigma$); see the commentary on thesis 33, above. Those who fictitiously interpret the word "practice" ($\pi\rho\hat{a}\xi\iota\varsigma$) as "virtuous action" are the same persons whom Ames opposes in thesis 34 for their interpretation of $\pi o i\eta\sigma\iota\varsigma$ as "perceptible to the senses." Even though Ames claims in the last sentence of thesis 93 that theology alone is responsible for teaching the universal precepts of virtue, he admits that virtuous action or its likeness may ultimately be observed in or outside the Church in any subject. But such observations are to be measured or judged "virtuous" or "a likeness of virtue" only according to the universal rules or precepts of theology. In theses 64 and 65 Ames has explained what he means by "likeness of virtue."

Thesis 94. Ames's degradation of the moral example of the pagans recalls his attack in theses 63–65 on excessive credulity in ancient and pagan writers. In thesis 94 the main burden of his argument does not rest on attacking the truth discerned by the untiring analysis of the pagan philosophers (that is, by attacking their so-called theoretical philosophy or poetic philosophy); rather, the burden of his argument rests on his attack on their practical or moral philosophy (that is, their "natural ethics"). The practical or moral philosophy of the ancient pagan philosophers mixes the teaching of virtues based on the obscured, corrupted sparks of the principles of goodness still shining in the type of things and in man's darkened conscience with the teaching of the virtues borrowed or imitated from the Hebrew Scriptures. But since even these imitations of the principles of virtue derived from the Hebrew Scriptures are only vestiges or spiritually dead images of virtue, the moral example of the pagans and the moral philosophy based on their example only makes up a body of corrupt and corrupting teaching, a mixture of "splendid sins." Ames concludes his attack on the division of the arts into theoretical and practical with the accusation that this division can and should be ascribed not to philosophers or theologians, who have been taught the principles of goodness and virtue from the Scriptures and by the supernatural illumination of the mind by the Holy Spirit, but rather to those pagans who are their imitators.

Thesis 95. Having now disposed of the defective division of the arts into theoretical and practical, Ames now turns to what he, in good Ramist fashion, regards as a "more true" division, grounded in the nature and essence of art. This discussion continues through the end of the second major section of *Technometry,* from thesis 95 to thesis 120. In this section Ames sets forth the division of the arts into general (subdivided into more and less) and special (subdivided into less and more); the order of the arts (the more general precede by nature and become concrete in the more specific); and the affections of the arts (seen in the logical etymologies or notations of the names of the six arts). Since he is laying out the whole body of the liberal arts curriculum, Ames properly closes this second section with a discussion in theses 118 and 119 of "encyclopedia," that is, "the circle of education."

Thesis 96. Ames sets forth the reasons (drawn from his arguments in the first major section of the treatise, theses 22–30, 55–60) for the "more true" division of art into general and special. Ames argues in thesis 96 that, since not only the object and end of art is divided into general and special but also its principles, art itself is most fittingly divided into general and special. The nature and essence of art expressed in terms of such a division is grounded in, harmonious with, and corroborative of its general definition. Ames proceeds to make explicit in the following theses what has been implicit or foreshadowed in the theses mentioned above and in this division of art into general and special.

Thesis 97. Following the pattern given in his discussion of general eupraxia, theses 23–26, Ames subdivides general art into more and less general. More general art is discussed in thesis 98; the less general arts are discussed in theses 99–103. The order and relations of the general arts to one another with respect to their use is discussed in thesis 104.

Thesis 98. Ames sets forth a concise, cryptic definition and distribution of dialectic; cf. the text of and commentary on thesis 23, above. Dialectic is distributed into invention, which "finds" or "discovers" the reasons or affections of things and puts them in their proper "places" or "regions." The reasons or affections of things are called "arguments" by the Ramists; for example, see Ames, *Demonstratio Logicae Verae,* thesis 4, p. 124. Ames admits in thesis 98 that dialectic has been taught genuinely from its own nature by "categories." But his qualified acceptance of the word "categories" in terms of the Ramist "arguments" shows that he had heeded Ramus's critique of Aristotle's categories and Ramus's replacement of the so-called Aristotelian predicaments and predicables by the one concept of "arguments." Ames explains what he means by "category" in *Demonstratio Logicae Verae,* thesis 28, p. 130; and he gives a Ramist critique of Aristotle's *Categories* in *Adversus Metaphysicam,* thesis 19, pp. 96–97. When Ames adds in his final statement of thesis 98 that dialectic utterly rejects any appendage of fallacies, he is rejecting the Aristotelian addition of sophistic or sophistical elenchies. Ramus held that, since logic is only concerned with the true guidance and use of reason, the teaching of falsehood and fallacies has no place in logical teaching. The judgment of truth or falsehood belongs to the second part of Ramist logic, namely, disposition or arrangement, which is called "judgment."

Thesis 99. Having briefly delineated in thesis 98 the definition and parts of the more general art of dialectic, Ames turns to the less general arts of grammar and rhetoric. The art of grammar is briefly and cryptically dealt with in theses 100–02, and the art of rhetoric is briefly and cryptically dealt with in thesis 103.

Thesis 100. The first of the less general arts is grammar. Ames gives a logical notation of the word "grammar" from the Greek verb γράφω, "I write." Even though Ramists defined grammar as "the art of speaking well" (*bene loquendi*), they intended that grammar include within itself not only pure and correct utterance but also pure and correct writing. This is made explicit when Ames says that "grammar" (*grammatica*) is derived "by synecdoche" from γράφω, that is, by means of the rhetorical trope of synecdoche whereby a part is set forth as if it were the whole. The inclusion of pure and correct utterance and pure and correct writing in the one art of grammar was a part of Ramus's reform of grammar over against either Varro or Quintilian. Both in his *Grammatica* and in his *Scholae Grammaticae Libri XX*, Ramus sets himself against Varro's division of grammar into etymology, analogy, and syntax and Quintilian's division of grammar into etymology, accent (*prosodia*), orthography, and syntax. Ramus claims that Varro's division breaks "the law of justice," while Quintilian's division breaks "the law of wisdom." Therefore, Ramus and his followers distribute grammar into etymology and syntax; see Ramus, *Grammatica,* bk. 1, chap. 1, p. 5.

Thesis 101. Ames gives expression to the still prevailing universality of the Latin language in the seventeenth century. Latin at this time was still the *lingua franca* and the language of the learned and academic world. The priority of the Latin language as the first of foreign tongues to be learned also implies the humanist passion for the Latin classics. In *Alia Technometriae Delineatio* the reason Ames gives for this translation of other languages into Latin is "so that they may be learned more quickly and more easily" (thesis 81, p. 67). Hence, Latin grammar is to be taught to students first and in terms of their own vernacular idiom. But once Latin grammar has been learned and after the student has gained some proficiency in the language by use and exercise, all other grammars (Hebrew, Greek, etc.) are to be taught in the Latin tongue, excepting only special and extraordinary words and usages that have no parallel in Latin.

Thesis 102. In *Alia Technometriae Delineatio* (thesis 82, pp.

67–68) Ames introduces the content that corresponds to thesis 102 with the following question: "Can the precepts of grammar and the precepts of the other arts be equally conformed to the three laws of the arts?" He answers this question in the negative, concluding that the precepts of grammar cannot be transmitted as normative for and accommodated to the laws of the remaining arts. There are two arguments that he gives for this conclusion. The first is that the precepts of grammar are determined to a great extent by their subject (that is, the substratum in which the precepts themselves adhere). The subject of the precepts of grammar is languages, which differ so greatly among themselves in method and common definitions (see thesis 101, above) and always involve so many individual exceptions to or irregularities in every rule that is set forth, that it is almost impossible to transmit precepts that can be regulative for and appropriated by the other arts. The second argument that Ames sets forth is that grammar, along with its associate, rhetoric, is merely a handmaiden (cf. thesis 26, above). The subordination of grammar and rhetoric to logic is further implied by Ames's statement that the eupraxia of discoursing well becomes concrete in other eupraxiae from *absolute necessity* (thesis 24), while the eupraxiae of speaking and communicating become concrete in other arts only by *hypothetical necessity* (thesis 25). The arts of grammar and rhetoric serve the subordinate function of communicating purely and ornately what has been perceived by man's reason in logic, namely, the reason, relation, and mutual affection of things along with the names or appellations of things (theses 56 and 57).

Thesis 103. The second of the less general arts is rhetoric. Ames gives a logical notation of the name "rhetoric" from the Greek verb ῥέω, "flow" (referring to "the flow of speech"), which he argues is derived from ἐρέω, "say" or "speak," and which he translates by the Latin verb *dico* (see the rhetorical meaning of *dico* in the commentary on thesis 25, above). Alsted has a similar passage that throws light on the logical "reason" for deriving "rhetoric" from these Greek verbs, although his final conclusion differs from that of Ames; see *Encyclopaedia,* vol. 1, bk. 7, chap. 1, p. 373. It has been pointed out above, in the commentary on thesis 98, that Ramus sets himself against the traditional division of rhetoric into invention, arrangement, style, memory, and delivery by making logic responsible for invention, arrangement, and memory, thereby leaving rhetoric responsible only for style (elocution) and delivery. This is the point at issue when Ames says that "in rhetoric the precepts of invention and disposition are repeated heterogeneously." In other words, rhetoric breaks the Ramist law of justice by usurping the teaching of invention and disposition or arrangement, which properly belongs to the art of logic. Ramus and his alter ego Omer Talon give the following definition and distribution of rhetoric: "Rhetoric is the art of communicating well. . . . There are two parts of rhetoric, elocution and pronunciation" (*Audomari Talaei Rhetorica, Ex P. Rami . . . Praelectionibus Observata* (Hanover, 1604), pp. 5–6. Ramists agreed that rhetoric is aimed primarily at the emotions or affects of men. But Ramist Puritans, such as Ames in thesis 25, always insisted on the subordination of rhetoric (and grammar) to logic. The logical axioms, uttered or written correctly according to grammatical precepts, are to be decorated by the tropes and figures, by the inflections of the voice and the gestures of the body, to make the oration sweet to the ears and eyes of the hearers. But such use or exercise of rhetoric must always be subservient to the truth demonstrated by logic insofar as it makes the path to truth pleasant, appealing, and sweet; cf. Richardson, *Rhetorical Notes,* p. 50.

Thesis 104. Following the pattern laid out in theses 24–26 regarding the three general eupraxiae and the division of general eupraxiae into more and less, Ames now makes his teaching more specific in the division of the individual arts. The more general art of logic and the less general arts of grammar and rhetoric become concrete in (that is, their precepts are appropriated or borrowed by) the remaining special arts of mathematics, physics, and theology. These latter three arts cannot be known without the art of logic, cannot be spoken correctly without the art of grammar, and cannot be communicated appropriately without the art of rhetoric.

Thesis 105. This discussion of the special arts of mathematics, physics, and theology must be understood in the light of theses

27–30, where Ames deals with the three special eupraxiae and their division. The arts of mathematics, physics, and theology have no use in the three general arts, nor do they become concrete in them; that is, their precepts are in no way appropriated or borrowed by the general arts. However, mathematics is less special because it becomes concrete in part with the art of physics; that is, it is used by physics (see the text of and commentary on theses 107–8, below). Physics and theology are more special because they become concrete in no other arts. Of the two more special arts, theology is the most special of all. This means that theology may sometimes borrow from the precepts of physics, but physics never borrows or uses the precepts of theology. The less special art of mathematics is dealt with in theses 106–8; the more special art of physics is dealt with in thesis 109; and the most special art of theology (the one in which Ames is most interested by profession and concern, as is witnessed by the number and length of the theses pertaining to it), is dealt with in theses 110–16.

Thesis 106. In deriving the name "mathematics" from the Greek verb μανθάνω, "I learn," Ames is following the lead of Ramus; see Ramus, *Scholarum Mathematicarum Liber IV*, p. 113. Ames's "reason" for this logical notation (namely, because boys once learned this art before the remaining arts to explore their natural talent and ability) has a strong echo of the Platonic doctrine of reminiscence that is so clearly expressed in such dialogues as the *Meno*. This association is made quite explicit by Ramus himself; see *Petri Rami Mathematicae Praefationes*, in *Collectaneae*, pp. 167–68. Ramus's and Ames's Aristotelian "empiricism," where there is nothing in the mind that has not first been in sense perception, leads them to reject this Platonic doctrine of reminiscence and its intimate association with mathematical science and forms. Nevertheless, overtones of the Platonic doctrine still come through in their logical notation of the word "mathematics." It has been noted above, in the commentary on thesis 30, that Ramus divided mathematics (the art of quantifying well) into arithmetic (the art of numbering well) and geometry (the art of measuring well). Ames defines mathematics as "the art of measuring well," and he does not discuss or even mention arithmetic in thesis 106 or in 107 and 108. However, in speaking of the use of mathematics by the less dignified faculties (that is, by the mechanical arts), he does mention in thesis 135 the "works" of mathematics: number, measure, and weight.

Thesis 107. Ames, following Ramus, rejects the distinction between abstract and concrete mathematics (see the commentary on thesis 35, above). In *Alia Technometriae Delineatio* (thesis 86, pp. 68–69) Ames clarifies the position that he is refuting in thesis 107: "Some commonly constitute one part of mathematics *abstract* from physics (such as cosmography, astronomy, geography, optics, music)." Alsted supports precisely the distinction that Ames is refuting here in *Encyclopaedia,* vol. 1, bk. 2, chap. 4, p. 65; see also *Encyclopaedia,* vol. 3, bk. 16, chaps. 1, 6, and bk. 17, chap. 1, pp. 962–63. For Ames, mathematics is a special art, but it is less special than physics and theology. This means that mathematics becomes concrete in part with the art of physics, that is, some of its precepts are borrowed by and accommodated to the use of the art of physics with respect to the dimensions of bodies (see thesis 30, above). But this does not mean that there are two mathematical arts. Rather, there is one less special mathematical art that is in part used by a more special art, thus verifying the theorem that posterior arts may use the precepts or the euprattomena of prior arts (see thesis 35, above). Ames would agree with Ramus in placing all of the examples of "concrete mathematics" within the jurisdiction of the art of physics. Other things that are often placed in this category belong neither to mathematics nor to physics but rather to the faculty or use of these arts. Ames mentions the faculty or use of mathematics in thesis 135 and the faculty or use of physics in theses 143–65, below.

Thesis 108. Once again Ames's failure to note arithmetic as part of mathematics is striking. It is in geometry, the art of measuring (*magnitude*) well, that the universal mathematical principles used by the parts of physics (mentioned in the commentary on thesis 107) are transmitted or taught. When he says that unuseful demonstrations are to be eliminated from geometry (or mathematics?) and that practice is to be primarily looked toward, Ames is once more affirming the central tenet of Ramism that all arguments and subtleties with no use for everyday living are empty and are to be excised from the arts; cf. Ramus, *Scholarum Mathematicarum Liber III,* p. 77.

Thesis 109. Ames gives a logical notation of the name "physics" from the Greek φύσις, "nature." His affirmation that physics ought to comprehend and pursue the whole nature of all natural being, in genus as much as in species, should be read in the light of the text of and commentary on thesis 54. Physics should deal not only with the general or primary essence of created things (which it receives or borrows from logical notation and definition) but also with the specific nature of individual things that have been differentiated, that is, with the *whole* nature of individual things. Ames's assertion in thesis 109 that physics ought to comprehend and pursue the *whole* nature of *all* natural or created being commits him to making physics responsible for teaching about incorporeal nature (such as angels and mind) as well as about corporeal nature made up of form and matter. Hence, he concludes that physics must comprehend the whole nature of those spiritual or incorporeal beings insofar as it is universally capable. This is an argument against those who held the view of Bartholomew Keckermann, who wanted a special art or science of "pneumatology" dealing with spirits; see *Scientiae Metaphysicae Brevissima Synopsis et Compendium,* bk. 1, chap. 15, in *Bartholomaei Keckermanni . . . Operum Omnium Quae Extant,* vol. 1, col. 2035. Ames's rejection of this special art or science of pneumatology and his inclusion of incorporeal nature as well as corporeal nature within the realm of the art of physics means that he also rejects the traditional definition of physics as "the science of contemplating natural body" (Keckermann) or simply as "the science of natural body" (Alsted). It may also be concluded that Ames, in his "Theses Physiologicae," holds a broader understanding of the concept "physiology" than does Alsted, who understands physiology to be the discipline considering natural body as part of the world. Ames's use of the word "physiology" is much closer to the broad sense mentioned by Ramus: "the reason of nature which the Greeks call physiology" (*Liber de moribus veterum Gallorum* [Paris, 1559], p. 46). Hence, the words "physics" and "physiology" are interchangeable terms for Ames. His exposition of the art of physics in

"Theses Physiologicae" shows how "traditional" he remained in his general understanding and elaboration of physics. He sets forth in these physical theses a basically Aristotelian psychology modified by certain voluntarist tendencies. In spite of the profession of his conviction that observation and experiment are needed for discovering and gathering the principles of the arts, especially in physics (see theses 70–72, above), Ames remains basically a "literary empiricist" in practice. Like Ramus before him, he mainly classifies and "methodizes" the prior works on physics by such authors as Aristotle, Lucretius, Pliny, Seneca, and Virgil.

Thesis 110. Ames comes to theology, the third and most special of the special arts (theses 110–16). He begins his discussion of theology, as he has begun his discussion of all the other arts, by giving a logical notation. He derives "theology" from the Greek words οἱ λόγοι τοῦ θεοῦ, which he translates "the declarations (*eloquii*) of God." *Eloquium* is a word used by the classical poets for *elocutio,* which in rhetorical language is used for "oratorical delivery or elocution." Hence, this translation of the Greek λόγοι by the Latin *eloquii* means that the οἱ λόγοι τοῦ θεοῦ may signify "striking rhetorical expressions" as well as "declarations" or "communications." It should be noted that Ames pluralizes the λογία in θεολογία to θεολογίαι and makes τοῦ θεοῦ a possessive (not an objective) genitive. Ames is here rejecting the interpretation of theology as the theory of speech *about* God and focuses attention upon God's revelation or declaration *of* his will in the Holy Scriptures. Ames declares that the principles of theology are no longer to be found primarily in the type of created things but in God's "declarations" in Holy Scripture. These "declarations" have the authority of testimony, and the divine testimony in Holy Scripture has the greatest authority of all because it has as its author the God of truth who cannot and does not lie. But since theology derives its principles from divine testimony or declarations (by means of the precepts of logic, grammar, and rhetoric), it cannot properly be called an art but is better called a (divine) teaching or doctrine; cf. *Marrow of Theology,* bk. 1, chap 1, theses 2–4, 9–10, 12, pp. 77–78.

Thesis 111. Ames asserts that theology, which derives its principles from the divine teaching in the Holy Scriptures, homogeneously (that is, legitimately or according to the law of justice) transmits the universal teaching about God. Ames, along with Calvin, holds that man cannot see God directly without being blinded and consumed. God has therefore accommodated himself to human reason by manifesting his wisdom, will, and glory in his creatures (that is, by revealing himself in "the book of nature"). But after the corruption and obscuration of the type of things in "the book of nature," especially that part of the type in which the principles of goodness shone, God has revealed his wisdom and will more clearly in "the book of Scripture." Hence, the obscurity and corruption of the book of nature is to be clarified and read in the clearer light of the book of Scripture. Even though God's revelation of his wisdom and will in the books of nature and Scripture does not include the knowledge of God's essence as he is in himself, and even though man can only know and speak about God either by arguing from effects to causes or by moving from one attribute to another, Ames contends that God's revelation of himself is still sufficient for man's living well, that is, living to God; see *Marrow of Theology,* bk. 1, chap. 4, theses 4–7, pp. 83–4.

Thesis 112. As Ames notes, he is drawing heavily in thesis 112 from his more extensive discussion of these matters in thesis 7 of his *Adversus Metaphysicam.* In that work he adds one significant aspect that does not come to light in thesis 112, namely, the assertion that "metaphysics is theoretical only, while theology is also practical" (*Adversus Metaphysicam,* thesis 7, p. 88). Ames has already attacked this distinction of arts or disciplines into theoretical and practical in theses 88–94, above. Ames's attack in thesis 112 may be taken as a general refutation of the Thomistic position with regard to the relation between human philosophy, which operates by the natural light of reason alone, and theology, which operates by supernatural light. Yet the emphasis on the word "metaphysics" and the claim that metaphysics is only speculative and practical both point to a more specific opponent, namely, the prolific Spanish Jesuit, Franciscus Suarez (1548–1617). The whole treatise *Adversus Metaphysicam* is in reality a discourse against Suarez, whose *Disputationes Metaphysicae* are mentioned or quoted over twenty times in the course of Ames's thirteen page treatise, including two references in thesis 7. The most relevant passage from Suarez (*Disputationes Metaphysicae,* bk. 1, chap. 5, thesis 5, in *Opera Omnia* [Paris, 1861], 25:38) draws together a series of the positions Ames is attacking in his *Technometry* and in thesis 7 of *Adversus Metaphysicam.* These positions include the distinction between speculative and practical sciences; the assertion that metaphysics and physics are only speculative or theoretical sciences; the "natural theology" claimed by metaphysics; and the distinction between the *kinds* of teachings about God based on the difference in the kinds of light (natural and supernatural) under which the human understanding proceeds to know him. Suarez formulates the concept of metaphysics that Ames castigates as vain and unuseful, the kind of "human wisdom" that is most severely punished by God; see thesis 91, above.

Thesis 113. Ames states the second responsibility of the "teaching" of theology, namely, that theology alone homogeneously (that is, legitimately or according to the law of justice) transmits the universal teachings of virtues. In thesis 62, above, Ames adds piety and justice to the list of virtues in thesis 113; namely, honesty, law, and equity. Ames elsewhere calls justice, defined generally as "an inclination to do rightly, giving every man his own," not only the "rectitude of virtue" but also the essential nature of virtue (*Marrow of Theology,* bk. 2, chap. 2, theses 24–26, p. 228). Ames conceives of virtue as a habit in the will, defining it as "a habit whereby the will is inclined to do well." Ames considers the will to be the proper subject of theology since the will is the proper principle of life and of moral and spiritual actions. It has been noted above, in the text of and commentary on thesis 110, that theology draws all of its principles (including those of virtues) from the divine teaching or revelation of God's will in the Holy Scriptures. Moreover, it has also been pointed out, in the texts of and commentaries upon theses 62 and 65, that the Holy Scriptures are the only sufficient rule and canon of life or of morals and law, that is, they set forth the *whole* revealed will of God for directing man's morals, will, and life. A full discussion of Ames's teaching about virtue would involve an analysis of the whole of book 2, "On Observance," of his *Marrow of Theology* and the entirety of his *Conscience*.

Thesis 114. In theses 114 and 115 Ames is arguing against the Peripatetic division of the practical sciences or prudences into ethics, household economy, and politics. For Aristotle, politics or the science of human affairs is the supreme practical science. Man is by nature a social being, and a social being can only achieve his good in a society that is organized for his welfare. The science of politics therefore has to discover first what the true happiness of man is and then the form of government and society that will secure that happiness for him. The first problem is dealt with in the *Nichomachean Ethics,* which is a study of man's ethos or character. The second problem is explained in the *Politics,* which is an investigation of the state. At the beginning of the *Politics,* Aristotle asserts that the state, the most supreme of all partnerships that includes all others, differs generically from the family, which is the primary association for the necessities of life (household economy). Related families form a city-state for the good life. The city-state, concludes Aristotle, is prior by nature to the household and to each individual person; for the whole must necessarily be prior to the part (*Politics* 1.1., p. 11). It has been noted above, in the text of and commentary on thesis 92, that Ames subsumes all of ethics, household economy, and politics under the teaching of theology; for all of the universal principles and precepts of these disciplines are borrowed from theology. They therefore do not make up any separate or distinct arts or sciences per se. Nor is jurisprudence a separate and distinct art or science. Thesis 113, above, notes that the principles and precepts of all the various kinds of law are *completely* revealed only in the Holy Scriptures. Hence, jurisprudence looks primarily to theology as the source of its universal principles and precepts, not to the more limited teachings of household economy (in Alsted's definition, "the prudence of establishing and administrating well a family") or politics (in Alsted's definition, "the prudence of establishing and administrating well a republic or commonwealth"). In thesis 123, below,

Ames describes the function of the "faculty" of jurisprudence as "proclaiming law and administering justice."

Thesis 115. This thesis draws upon the arguments given and analyzed in the texts of and commentaries on theses 63–65 and 94. Jurisprudence has no need of ethics; in fact, these is no need for ethics or moral philosophy at all.

Thesis 116. The noun translated as "pretexts" (*praetextii*) comes from the verb *praetexo,* which literally means "to weave before or in front," and figuratively comes to mean "to allege as an excuse," "to pretend," "to assign as a pretext." The verb translated as "have been rewoven" is from *retexo,* which can mean both "to unweave" or "to unravel" and also (the direct opposite) "to weave again or anew," "to renew or repeat." All of these words are derived from the basic verb *texo,* which literally means simply "to weave or plait." The image that arises from Ames's language here is that of ethicists who have woven together certain pretenses that, after having been unravelled and shown to be what they are by such arguments as he has given in theses 63–65, 92, and 113–15, are often rewoven or repeated again by the ethicists who continue to hold the Aristotelian position. Thesis 116 and a large part of Ames's *Adversus Ethicam* are a direct attack upon the position represented by Bartholomew Keckermann in his *Systematis Ethici Praecognita Generalia.* In thesis 25 of his *Adversus Ethicam* (pp. 112–13), Ames has a passage that briefly touches upon some of the positions and arguments expounded here in thesis 116; he has a longer passage that more nearly resembles thesis 116 in his *Marrow of Theology,* bk. 2, chap. 2, thesis 17, p. 226. Ames begins his attack by quoting a passage from Keckermann that distinguishes the end of ethics from the end of sacred theology; see *Systematis Ethici Praecognita Generalia,* paragraphs 1–6, in *Opera Omnia* (Geneva, 1614), vol. 2, cols. 251–52. Ames refutes this position with four arguments that, it should be noted, do not reject the thesis that man's highest good is beatitude or happiness. The second "pretext" of the ethicists is a position clearly expressed by Keckermann in *Systematis Ethici Praecognita Generalia,* par. 12, col. 254, as are the third and fourth in par. 10, col. 253. With regard to the fifth position of the ethicists, Keckermann does not draw upon Matthew 5:20, Matthew 6 and 7, or Romans 1 and 2; rather, he draws upon 1 Timothy 2:1–2 as the divine authority for a distinction between ethical and theological virtues (*Systematis Ethici Praecognita Generalia,* par. 10, cols. 253–54). Ames argues that nothing about such a distinction between ethical and theological virtues is to be found in these texts.

Thesis 117. Ames has now completed the main purpose of the second major section (theses 88–120) of his treatise on *Technometry,* namely, setting forth the nature or essence of art in its division into general and special. He has generally set forth the definitions or notations and something about the content of the three general arts (logic, grammar, and rhetoric) and each of the three special arts (mathematics, physics, and theology). He concludes this second major section with a brief discussion of how these arts are related in man (thesis 117), in encyclopedia (theses 118–19), and among themselves in order of primacy (thesis 120). Ames's use of the phrase "the whole man" in thesis 117 shows that he conceives of this phrase as including man's intellect, his will, and his locomotion. What Ames means by the remaining four arts of grammar, rhetoric, mathematics, and physics "perfecting man's locomotion according to rule in their eupraxiae" is clarified by a passage from Keckermann; see *Systematis Ethici Praecognita Generalia,* col. 270. Ames is not speaking in thesis 117 of the locomotion that man shares in common with all animals (discussed in chap. 53 of his "Theses Physiologicae") but the more particularly restricted locomotion of man that is governed by intellect and will. The precepts of these four arts, known by the intellect, become the rules that govern the will and thereby guide man's external activity or locomotion.

Thesis 118. Thesis 117 provides the premise from which the conclusion is drawn in thesis 118; cf. *Alia Technometriae Delineatio,* thesis 89, pp. 69–70. Alsted gives an analysis of the use of the word "encyclopedia" that helps in interpreting Ames's use of the word; see Alsted, *Encyclopaedia,* vol. 1, bk. 1, chap. 1, p. 49. It is clear that Ames understands the word in the narrower sense of "the circle of liberal arts" that, under the guidance of

Ramus, has been modified and reduced to six rather than the seven of the medieval *trivium* and *quadrivium*. What Ames means by defining "encyclopaedia" as the circular comprehension of the six arts in relation to the emanation of all things from and their return to First Being is clarified by the much fuller discussion in Richardson, *The Logicians School-Master*, pp. 14–15, 17. For Richardson and for Ames, logic or dialectic (the most universal art) is the first link of the circular chain of encyclopedia, grammar is the second, rhetoric the third, mathematics the fourth, physics the fifth, and theology (the most special of all the arts) is the sixth and last link. Ames argues that he has made it clear that the chain of encyclopedia has neither more nor less than these six arts by excluding those disciplines that others try in vain to include as arts (such as metaphysics, ethics, household economy, politics, and jurisprudence), and by correctly enumerating and attributing the objects and the laws of the true arts. He promises that he will make this even clearer in what follows; see theses 119, 121, 123–24, 126–29, 132, 135 below.

Thesis 119. Ames lists the four precognitions or preliminary disciplines that comprise volume 1 of Alsted's *Encyclopaedia*. These four precognitions, which Alsted defines as instruction preparing the mind of a learner or pupil for an easier grasping or comprehension of the discipline or disciplines that are about to be taught, include the following: archelogy ("the teaching which is to be foreknown about the principles of all the disciplines"); hexiology ("the teaching which is to be foreknown about the intellectual habits by means of which a man is disposed to understand intelligible things, with respect to principles or conclusions which are set forth for the sake of cognition or of action"); technology ("the teaching which is to be foreknown about the affections, order, and division of the disciplines"); and didactic ("the teaching which is to be foreknown about the study of the disciplines in general and in specific"). Ames mentions that others try to force (in addition to these four precognitions) eleven sciences, five prudences, and seven arts into the circle of encyclopedia. Although Alsted is by no means the only one whom Ames is opposing, he may be taken as representative of that group. Alsted distinguishes between and deals with eleven theoretical sciences, six practical prudences, and nine poetic arts. Ames claims that some of the disciplines listed by Alsted beyond the six true arts break the law of justice when they claim to be arts, while others are only improperly called "arts" by metonymy (see thesis 122, below). With regard to Alsted's four precognitions, Ames claims that archelogy (see theses 42–81, above) and hexiology (see theses 43, 79, 80, 84–87, above) are included within his own broader understanding of technology or technometry. Since technology is not a separate or independent art but rather draws its principles and universal precepts from those six arts, it (and therefore archelogy and hexiology) is not a link in the chain of encyclopedia. Furthermore, since didactic is only an external adjunct (that is, not a part of the primary essence or nature) of technology or technometry, it is even further removed from the circle of encyclopedia than is technology.

Thesis 120. Ames concludes the second major section of his *Technometry* by showing how three of the six arts that make up encyclopedia "contend" for primacy. Theology, logic, and grammar can all three claim to be "first," but they are first in different senses; cf. Ramus's order of study for his students in *Pro Philosophica Parisiensis academiae disciplina, Oratio,* in *Collectaneae,* p. 336. Ames argues that grammar is first in conformity with man's manner of advancing in learning. He has argued in theses 24 and 104 that logic or dialectic is first by absolute necessity, for all of the other arts can only be known by man's reason, which is perfected by the art of logic. But theology is first in dignity, both because it is derived from the infallible testimony of God himself and also because it has to do with man's will (that is, the act of the *whole* man) and life, the most noble of all acts (see *Marrow of Theology,* bk. 1, chap. 1, thesis 4, p. 77). Therefore, although theology is the most special of all the arts and the last art to be taught in the universities, it is still the most noble and dignified of all.

Thesis 121. Ames turns to the third and final section, or more accurately, the second part of his first major distribution of technometry, namely, the use in general of all the arts and of every individual art (theses 121–69). Ames argues in thesis 121 that no finite man can possibly use or exercise all of the arts in every way; therefore there has been a specialization of tasks and responsibilities wherein various artificers acquire faculties (that is, skills or capabilities for doing things easily and well) of using the arts or some art in various kinds of life, with respect to various objects, and for various ends that are useful for human life. Ames argues that these uses of the arts and "faculties" for using them are only improperly and by metonymy called "arts." This improper terminology is grounded in a metonymy of an effect for the cause, as becomes clear in theses 133 and 135, where Ames states that the less dignified faculties are "effects" of the arts of mathematics, physics, and grammar.

Thesis 122. Ames distributes the "faculties" of using the arts into those that are "more dignified" and "less dignified." He discusses the "more dignified" faculties of using the arts in theses 123–30 and the "less dignified" faculties in theses 131–66. In theses 131 and 132 Ames explains that the artificers and also the objects and ends they pursue are "more or less dignified." In thesis 122 he further subdivides the "more dignified" faculties of using the arts into "higher" (dealt with in theses 123–26) and "lower" (dealt with in theses 127–30). In thesis 127 he explains the way in which the more dignified higher faculties surpass or excell the more dignified lower faculty.

Thesis 123. By calling the uses of the arts "faculties," Ames is able to relate the use of the arts to the teaching of the arts by various faculties of the universities (that is, by various teachers of the arts who transmit and practice the various arts). The "more dignified faculties," dealt with in theses 123–32, are none other than the various skills acquired by teachers or men learned in the "liberal" or "literate" arts and in the three higher disciplines of theology, jurisprudence or law, and medicine. The relation of Ames's discussion of the more dignified faculties to the arts curriculum of the universities is confirmed in thesis 168, below, where he discusses the various academic degrees awarded by the universities. In thesis 123 Ames begins with a summary statement of the three higher faculties and their objects or ends. The juridical faculty is further elaborated upon in theses 124 and 125, the medical faculty in thesis 126.

Thesis 124. Ames states that the jurisprudence contained in the

Corpus Juris or Roman Law and any other writings on the civil laws is to be treated in this "place," namely, under the heading of the more dignified, higher faculties, and more specifically under the higher faculty of jurisprudence. Ames's emphasis upon the *Corpus Juris* shows how important this work remained for the study of jurisprudence in Ames's day. What Ames means by "the reasons that are the force and soul of the laws" is clarified below in thesis 125 in the quotation from the "jurisconsult," Antoine Favre. When Ames states that neither the *Corpus Juris* nor any other writings on the civil law transmit the universal principles of law, but, rather, theology alone homogeneously transmits such principles, he is drawing upon his argument in theses 113–15, above.

Thesis 125. Ames quotes a passage from the jurisconsult (that is, a man learned in the law, especially international law), Antonius Fabrius (1557–1624), better known by his French name, Antoine Favre; see *Iurisprudentiae Papinianeae Scientia, ad Ordinem Institutionum Imperialium efformata,* vol. 1, bk. 2, chap. 5 (Lyons, 1607), p. 9. Ames uses this quotation to argue that a jurisconsult can only be prudent (that is, can only discern the right means for exercising his understanding, science, and wisdom) when he knows the law's force and power (that is, the reason of law depending on the principles of law). It is not enough for a jurisconsult to know only the letter or words of the law. The prudent jurisconsult must first understand the universal principles and precepts of law transmitted by the art of theology. Ames concludes thesis 125 by saying that this quotation from Favre may be applied not only to jurisconsults, who derive their principles of law from the art of theology, but also—after the name of the artificers or workers and the arts from which they derive their first principles have been changed—to the other more dignified faculties. The faculties to which Favre's quotation also applies include the following group: physicians and medical writers, who derive their first principles from the art of physics (thesis 126); philosophers, who primarily derive their first principles from the arts of rhetoric, physics, and theology (thesis 128); and workers, who possess the less dignified (that is, the mechanical or manual) faculties and who derive a few of their first principles from the art of mathematics, some from the art of grammar, and most from the art of physics (thesis 133).

Thesis 126. Ames asserts that medicine and all other kinds of medical writings are to be taught in this "place," which is concerned with the more dignified, higher faculties, and more specifically in the place concerned with the medical faculty. Ames had in his library various works on alchemy, chemistry, pharmacy, and the structure of the human body as well as various general treatises on practical medicine; see *Catalogus,* pp. 13–14. The fact that physicians prescribe various drugs for restoring man's health means that medicine is also intimately related to the less dignified faculty of the pharmacist, who makes or mixes the various drugs (see thesis 165, below). Ames's reference to physics considered in its complete being rather than in its defective existence should be read in the light of the imperfection of the eupraxia of the art of physics, mentioned above in thesis 31, and the reasons for that imperfection, discussed in theses 71 and 72.

Thesis 127. There are two different senses that may be discerned in Ames's use of the phrase "lower faculty" when referring to the philosophical faculty. The first sense has nothing derogatory in it but rather reflects the typical way of speaking of the arts curriculum and the various faculties of teachers in the universities. Before and during Ames's time the learning of grammar, rhetoric, and philosophy were the course of study for the advanced study of theology, jurisprudence, or medicine. There is a second and more derogatory sense, however, that can be discerned in Ames's speaking of the philosophical faculty as "lower." This more derogatory sense can be seen in the way in which he handles the logical notation or derivation of the word philosophy. When Ames speaks of the philosophical faculty being "lower" because it belongs to those who are only lovers of the wisdom that they have not yet attained but that is attained by the higher faculties, he is in a sense looking down upon the "lower" and indeed "inferior" faculty. Part of this putting philosophy into its proper (that is, "lower") place is certainly to be explained by Ames's conflict with the philosophy and philosophers of his own and previous times. He greatly restricts the breadth and scope of philosophy (see theses 128–129), and he rejects the traditional divisions of philosophy *either* into theoretical and practical *or* into theoretical, practical, and poetical. He furthermore has rejected the basic philosophical disciplines of metaphysics and ethics. Yet, in spite of Ames's sharp delimitation of the scope and responsibility of philosophy, he by no means totally rejected it or its usefulness. He only reinterpreted and restricted the meaning of the term, and he made philosophy a faculty of using the precepts derived from other arts rather than an art per se.

Thesis 128. It is noteworthy that there is no mention of logic, grammar, or mathematics in Ames's list of the seven partial faculties making up the philosophical faculty. Ames thinks of the art of logic as common to all the other arts and as the art from which the philosophical *and* the higher faculties draw some of their principles. He does not include grammar and mathematics because he wishes to elaborate upon their application in the less dignified faculties (see thesis 133, below). Ames, like Ramus, regards optics and music as belonging to the art of physics. It is striking that Ames makes architecture, the faculty of building well, a part of the more dignified, lower, philosophical faculty rather than the less dignified, mechanical, illiberal faculties. It should also be noted in this context that the idea or form of a house preexisting in the mind of an architect is one of Ames's favorite models for understanding art (see thesis 4, above).

Thesis 129. Ames assigns a number of different "systems" to the lower philosophical faculty. Philosophers exercise their faculty in drawing forth philosophical conclusions by accommodation of the universal precepts of the arts of rhetoric, physics, and theology.

Thesis 130. In spite of the fact that Ames has expelled all of the philosophical systems mentioned in thesis 129 from the circle of arts properly so-called, he includes this thesis to stress the usefulness and even the necessity of these systems that "survey" the philosophical faculty. The reading and cognition of these systems makes it easier to acquire more correctly the whole philosophical faculty and also the three higher faculties of theology, jurisprudence, and medicine.

Thesis 131. Ames has now dealt with the more dignified, liberal faculties of using the arts, namely, the theological, the juridical, the medical, and the philosophical. In theses 131–66 he finally turns his attention to the less dignified faculties for using the arts.

Thesis 132. There are passages similar to thesis 132 in Alsted, who by contrast makes these "mechanical arts" a part of the circle of encyclopedia; see *Encyclopaedia*, vol. 7, bk. 18, chap. 1, p. 1,861. Alsted agrees with Ames in being somewhat uneasy about the customary nomenclature that tends to villify the less dignified faculties (Ames) or the mechanical arts (Alsted); see Alsted, *Encyclopaedia*, vol. 6, bk. 28, chap. 1, p. 1,860. What Ames means by some of these less dignified faculties being more liberal while others are more servile and base is clarified in thesis 166, below. Ames's argument for the dignity and usefulness per se of the less dignified faculties (theses 132–34) should be related to his Protestant teaching about work; see, for example, *Marrow of Theology*, bk. 2, chap. 20, theses 24–28, pp. 322–23.

Thesis 133. The Ramist teaching about "effect" states that effects exist from the four causes; and "since the force of a cause is present in the effect, it is truly said that 'the caused is of the same kind as the cause,' namely, with respect to that power which the caused receives from the cause" (Ames, *Theses Logicae*, thesis 31, p. 163). Therefore, since the arts of mathematics, physics, and grammar are the causes of the less dignified faculties, nothing should be attributed to these less dignified faculties that should not also be attributed to these three arts.

Thesis 134. In terms of Ramist logic, a contradiction is an argument that is a dissenting, negative contrary; see *Demonstratio Logicae Verae*, theses 42–43, pp. 134–35. Ames is presupposing in thesis 134 that anything *truly* useful or necessary for society is commanded by God and is therefore virtuous or just.

Thesis 135. Ames elaborates upon what he says in thesis 133 when he affirms that the less dignified faculties are the effects of the arts of mathematics, physics, and grammar. In thesis 135 he analyzes the less dignified faculties in terms of three of the four Aristotelian-scholastic causes, omitting a discussion only of *efficient causation*. Physics or grammar is the *final cause* of the less dignified faculties because these faculties imitate physics or grammar as their idea and model. Mathematics is the *formal cause* of all the less dignified faculties because these faculties imitate the works of mathematics (namely, number, measure, and weight) that make up the just proportion of the parts in which there is the being of form. Physics or grammar is the *material cause* of the less dignified faculties because these faculties borrow their matter or material from one or the other of these two arts. When Ames says that the mechanical faculties borrow the *principal* object of their exercise from the arts of physics or grammar, he means that the mechanical faculties have as their principal object either doing the work of nature well or speaking (which includes writing) well or correctly.

Thesis 136. Ames elaborates upon the conclusion reached at the end of thesis 135. In spite of his criticism in thesis 121 of the use of the word "arts" with respect to the uses of the arts or the faculties of using the arts, Ames here, by metonymy of the effect for the cause, uses the more traditional terminology in calling the less dignified faculties "mechanical arts." He distributes the less dignified faculties or mechanical arts into grammatical (which are concerned about grammatical things and are dealt with in theses 137–42) and into physical (which are concerned with physical things and are dealt with in theses 143–65).

Thesis 137. Ames further subdivides the grammatical faculties into those that are concerned with forming letters in customary figures or letters by pen (treated in thesis 138) or by type (treated in thesis 139), or into those faculties that are concerned about forming letters in uncustomary figures (treated in theses 140 and 141).

Thesis 138. "Calligraphy" (*calligraphia*) is a transliteration into Latin from the Greek καλλιγραφία, which is made up of καλά, "beautiful" or "of fine quality," and γραφία, "writing." Hence, "calligraphy" may mean either "beautiful writing" (whether of figures or style) or "fine penmanship." Ames includes both meanings in thesis 138.

Thesis 139. "Typography" (*typographia*) is a transliteration into Latin of the Greek τύπος, which primarily means "a blow" or "the effect of a blow" and secondarily "an impression," and from the Greek γραφία, "writing." The word "typography" can best be translated as "writing by type." Ames was writing at the time of the crest of the wave caused by Gutenberg's discovery of printing by metallic type; cf. Alsted's definition of typography as "the art by means of which the concepts of men are by metallic letters and ink imprinted with astonishing swiftness on paper" (*Encyclopaedia*, vol. 6, bk. 30, chap. 1, p. 1,913). The Latin word *libraria*, translated freely in thesis 139 as "bookmanship," is derived from the Latin *liber*, which most frequently means "a book" but in its primary sense means "the bark or rind of trees." *Libraria* embraces both the faculty of the bookbinder and that of the librarian.

Thesis 140. Brachygraphy (*brachygraphia*) is a transliteration into Latin from the Greek noun βραχύς, "a short time or space," and γραφία, "writing." It is best translated into modern usage as "writing in shorthand." Brachygraphy was and still is used not only to save time but also to save space. The best examples of brachygraphy are to be found in late medieval manuscripts written in abbreviated Latin and in many of the texts printed in the fifteenth, sixteenth, and early seventeenth centuries.

Thesis 141. The so-called "art" of ciphers means "writing in code." Ames sets forth two possibilities for acquiring and exercising such an art or faculty, both of which are discussed by Francis Bacon (Baron Verulam) in *Of the Dignity and Advancement of Learning*, bk. 6, chap. 1, in *The Works of Francis Bacon* (Boston, 1864), 9:116–17.

Thesis 142. *Chartopoeia*, "paper-making," is a transliteration into Latin from the Greek χάρτης, which originally meant "a leaf of the Egyptian papyrus plant," and the Greek verb ποιέω, "make" or "produce." *Pergamenopoeia*, parchment-making, is derived from the same Greek verb and the name of the Greek city Πέργαμον, Pergamum in Mysia; for parchment, a material for writing prepared from the skins of animals, was once invented by Eumenes, king of Pergamum. Thesis 142 shows that not only the arts but also the less dignified faculties are hierarchically ordered and mixed in their use; the faculty of making paper or parchment is subordinate to and serves the other grammatical faculties that are treated in theses 138–41.

Thesis 143. In theses 143–65 Ames discusses the less dignified, physical faculties. These theses follow the general order of chapters 13–40 of his "Theses Physiologicae." Alexander Richardson discusses the distinction between the elements and things composed of the elements in *Notes on Physicks* (London, 1657), pp. 108–09. Ames gives his own general discussion of the elements in *Theses Physiologicae,* chap. 13, theses 1–5, 7–8, p. 40. In thesis 143 Ames mentions the physical faculties concerned with fire (dealt with in thesis 144), air (dealt with in thesis 145), water (dealt with in thesis 146), and earth (dealt with in thesis 147). The physical faculties concerned with the qualities of the elements are discussed in thesis 148. The physical faculties concerned with the qualities of things composed of the elements are treated in thesis 149; and the physical faculties concerned with the things themselves composed of the elements are treated in theses 150–65.

Thesis 144. Ames sets forth the species of physical faculties that are concerned with the element of fire. The genus that includes all of these species is *pyrotechnia,* "the art of fire"; see *Alia Technometriae Delineatio,* thesis 109, p. 75. Alsted gives a full definition and outline of the general "art" of pyrotechnia in *Encyclopaedia,* vol. 6, bk. 35, chap. 7, p. 2,284.

Thesis 145. Ames sets forth the species of physical faculties that are concerned with the element of air. The genus of all these specific faculties is *aerotechnia,* "the art of air"; see *Alia Technometriae Delineatio,* thesis 110, p. 76.

Thesis 146. Ames sets forth the species of physical faculties that are concerned with the element of water. The genus of all these specific faculties is hydrography (*hydrographia*); see *Alia Technometriae Delineatio,* thesis 111, p. 76. Alsted has an extensive discussion of the nautical art in *Encyclopaedia,* vol. 6, bk. 30, chap. 7, pp. 1,927–29.

Thesis 147. Ames here gives no genus of the species of physical faculties that are concerned with the element of earth. He can only argue that "a certain part" of agriculture and of gardening is in these faculties; for the more important or essential part of the faculty of gardening is concerned with herbage, just as the faculty of agriculture has to do with sowing seeds and cultivating fruits in the ear (see thesis 159).

Thesis 148. Ames sets forth the physical faculties concerned not with the elements themselves but rather with their primary and secondary qualities. He has a rather extensive discussion of these qualities in "Theses Physiologicae," chap. 17, theses 1–6, and chap. 18, theses 1–9, pp. 40–41. The primary qualities of the elements have to do with heat and cold, which are *primarily* in the elements themselves; the element of fire is the hottest and most noble, the element of water is the coldest, while the elements of air and earth are somewhere in between. The secondary qualities of the elements are either derived from the effects of the primary qualities or from the proportionate amount of matter and form in the different elements.

Thesis 149. Ames lists the physical faculties that are concerned with the qualities of things composed of the elements. Ames lists these faculties under the rubric of the five external senses of perception, although he lists no qualities concerned with touch; cf. "Theses Physiologicae," chap. 49, theses 1–2, p. 48. Painting is here classified as one of the less dignified, physical faculties (that is, as a mechanical art). Painting (whether of a house or a canvas) had not yet escaped the stigma of being associated with manual and corporal labor. Music is referred by Ames to the more dignified, lower philosophical faculty (see theses 128–29, above). But the faculties of playing musical instruments involve corporal and manual labor, and they must be taught by apprenticeship or by the manual transmission of another artisan. Hence, Ames sets forth in thesis 149 a long list of musical instruments that were popular in his time. In *Alia Technometriae Delineatio* (thesis 116, p. 77), he also includes dancing as a physical faculty that is concerned with sound. The faculty of cooking is in some way concerned with herbage, as is that of the florist (see thesis 159, below).

Thesis 150. Ames prepares to discuss the physical faculties concerned with the things composed of the elements. He distributes these faculties into those that are concerned with inanimate things (theses 151–57) and living things (theses 158–65). The faculties concerned with inanimate stones are dealt with in thesis 151, those concerned with inanimate metals in theses 152–56, and those concerned with inanimate minerals of a median nature in thesis 157. Those faculties that are concerned with living things are either concerned with plants (thesis 159) or with animals (theses 160–65).

Thesis 151. Ames lists the physical faculties that are concerned with stones; cf. his discussion of stones in "Theses Physiologicae," chap. 34, theses 1–4, p. 44.

Thesis 152. Ames lists the physical faculties that are concerned with metals. The genus of all the faculties concerned with specific metals is "metallurgy"; see Alsted, *Encyclopaedia,* vol. 6, bk. 29, chap. 8, p. 1,909.

Thesis 153. Ames lists the physical faculties concerned with gold and silver.

Thesis 154. Ames lists the physical faculties concerned with bronze.

Thesis 155. Ames lists the physical faculties concerned with iron.

Thesis 156. Ames lists the physical faculties concerned with copper, tin, and lead.

Thesis 157. Ames lists the physical faculties concerned with minerals, which have a median nature between stones and metals.

Thesis 158. Having completed his discussion of the physical faculties that are concerned with inanimate things, Ames now focuses upon the physical faculties that are concerned with living things animated by a vegetable soul (that is, plants, dealt with in thesis 159), by a vegetative and animal soul (that is, animals, dealt with from theses 160–64), or by a vegetative, animal, and rational soul (that is, man, who is dealt with in thesis 165).

Thesis 159. Ames lists the physical faculties that are concerned with plants; cf. his discussion of plants in general in "Theses Physiologicae," chap. 36, theses 1–3, 5–7, p. 45. See also *Alia Technometriae Delineatio,* theses 123–26.

Thesis 160. Ames turns to the second part of living things, namely, animals. He turns first to brute or irrational animals (theses 160–64). Cf. Ames's discussion about animals in general ("Theses Physiologicae," chap. 36, theses 1–3, 5–7, p. 45) and about brute animals in particular ("Theses Physiologicae," chap. 39, p. 46).

Thesis 161. Ames lists the physical faculties concerned with birds.

Thesis 162. Ames lists the physical faculties concerned with fish.

Thesis 163. Ames lists the physical faculties concerned with domestic, terrestrial animals. Here again the hierarchy of the various faculties of the arts becomes apparent.

Thesis 164. Ames lists the physical faculties concerned with wild, terrestrial animals.

Thesis 165. Ames lists the physical faculties concerned with man's body; cf. his general discussion of man, his body, and his soul in "Theses Physiologicae," chap. 40, theses 1–6, and chap. 41, theses 1–7, p. 46. Alsted's discussion of pharmacy, surgery, and anatomy (*Encyclopaedia*, vol. 29, bk. 8, p. 1909) throws light upon Ames's mention of the physical faculties that are concerned with healing man's body.

Thesis 166. Ames has now set forth in general art's use in those faculties that are more dignified (theses 123–30) and those that are less dignified (theses 131–65). He makes no claim to completeness in his listing of all the faculties of using the six arts enumerated and briefly described in the second major section of this treatise (theses 88–120); cf. *Alia Technometriae Delineatio*, thesis 135, p. 81). Ames again implies that the faculties that have been acquired from known and applied precepts of the arts dignify the artisans who possess them more than those faculties that have only been acquired from written transmission or from transmission through the hands of other artificers.

Thesis 167. Ames concludes this final section on art's use in general in the more or less dignified faculties by asking: "After someone has acquired for himself one of these faculties, by what right (*jure*) does he use it?" (*Alia Technometriae Delineatio*, thesis 136, p. 81). He answers this question with respect to candidates of the more dignified faculties in thesis 168, and with respect to candidates of the less dignified faculties in thesis 169. He begins thesis 167 by giving two reasons for having academic degrees in the universities and trial works in the trade guilds. The first reason is negative, namely, so that a person cannot vainly claim to have acquired some faculty and do some harm to himself, his neighbor, or society. The second reason is positive, namely, because every man ought to be productive (that is, ought to be occupied in some work that is in conformity with the will of God and with the benefit of mankind).

Thesis 168. This thesis demonstrates how intimately this whole treatise on *Technometry* is bound up with teaching, pedagogical techniques, and the stages of the teaching and learning process; cf. *Alia Technometriae Delineatio,* thesis 137, p. 81. Many Puritans who received degrees (especially in theology) did not make a career of teaching in the universities but became pastors of churches instead. Yet even here they were recognized and honored as members of a learned teaching ministry.

Thesis 169. Ames gives a somewhat fuller statement of this thesis in *Alia Technometriae Delineatio,* thesis 138, p. 82. The word *tyrocinium* not only means "a trial work" but also "noviceship." The German word *Meisterstück* literally means "a masterpiece." Ames is referring here to an apprentice who has to make at the end of his apprenticeship a satisfactory trial work or masterpiece to demonstrate that he has acquired sufficient skill in his trade to become a master craftsman in his own right and that he is qualified to become a member of his own trade guild.

Index

Abbot, George, 5

aerotechnia, 194

Agricola, Rudolf, 23

agriculture, 121, 194

Alsted, John Henry, 29–30, 31, 42, 47, 48, 74 n. 56, 83 n. 93, 150, 184–86

Ames, John (son), 65 n. 7

Ames, Ruth (daughter), 65 n. 7

Ames, William (father), 4

Ames, William: childhood of, 4; at Christ's College, 4–5; escape to Holland, 5; dispute with John Robinson, 6–7; chaplain at The Hague, 6–8; controversy with Arminians, 6–8; second wife and children of, 7, 17; at University of Franeker, 10–16; called to New England, 15; called to Rotterdam church, 15–16; death of, 16; influence of, 41; significance of, vii–viii; library of, 41, 74 n. 53, 79 n. 75; writings: "Alia technometriae delineatio," 13, 78 n. 72; *Anti-Synodalia Scripta*, 11; *Bellarminus Enervatus*, 11; *Christianae catecheseos*, 11; *Coronis ad Collationem Hagiensem*, 8, 65 n. 8; *De Arminii Sententia*, 7; *De Conscientia* (*Conscience, Cases of Conscience*), 11, 12, 16, 48, 51, 66–67 n. 15, 79 n. 74, 163; "Demonstratio logicae verae," 13, 46; "Disputatio theologica adversus metaphysicam," 13, 44, 78 n. 72, 112–13, 180–81; "Disputatio theologica, de perfectione SS. Scripturae," 13, 44, 78 n. 72, 113–15, 155, 183; *Explicatio Analytica Epistolae Petri*, 11; *Lectiones in CL. Psalmos*, 11; *Manuduction for Mr. Robinson*, 7; *Medulla Theologiae* (*Marrow of Theology*), 9, 10, 11, 16, 46, 48, 51, 66 n. 9, n. 10, 79 n. 74, 83 n. 93; *Opera Omnia*, 13; "Paranesis ad Studios," 10; *Philosophemata*, 12–14; preface to Baynes, *The Diocesans Tryall*, 9; preface to Bradshaw, *Puritanismus Anglicanus*, 5; *Reply to Dr. Mortons Particular Defence*, 10; *Rescriptio Scholastica*, 7; *Second Manuduction for Mr. Robinson*, 7; "Technometria," ix–x, 13, 14, 78 n. 72; "Theses logicae," 13, 83 n. 93; "Theses Physiologicae," 14, 46, 140, 178–79, 194

Ames, William, Jr. (son), 7, 65 n. 7

Amesians, 6

Amesius, Guilielmus. *See* Ames, William